St. Jerome Publishing
Manchester, UK & Kinderhook (NY), USA

First published 2002, and reprinted 2007 by
St. Jerome Publishing
2 Maple Road West, Brooklands
Manchester, M23 9HH, United Kingdom
Tel +44 161 973 9856
Fax +44 161 905 3498
stjerome@compuserve.com
http://www.stjerome.co.uk

ISBN-10: 1-900650-54-1 (pbk) ISBN-13: 978-1-900650-54-0 (pbk)

Printed and bound in Great Britain by T. J. International Ltd., Cornwall, UK

Cover design by
Steve Fieldhouse, Oldham, UK (+44 161 620 2263)

Typeset by
Delta Typesetters, Cairo, Egypt
Email: hilali1945@hotmail.com

British Library Cataloguing in Publication Data
A catalogue record of this book is available from the British Library

Library of Congress Cataloging-in-Publication Data
Williams, Jenny.
 The Map : a beginner's guide to doing research in translation studies
/ by Jenny Williams and Andew Chesterman.
    p.cm.
Includes bibliographical references and index.
  ISBN-10: 1-900650-54-1 (Paperback : alk. paper)
  ISBN-13: 978-1-900650-54-0 (Paperback : alk. paper)
  1. Translating and interpreting--Research--Methodology. I. Chesterman,
Andrew. II. Title.
  P306.5 .W547 2002
  418'02'072--dc21
                          2002000072

Contents

Acknowledgements		*v*
Introduction		1
1.	Areas in Translation Research	6
2.	From the Initial Idea to the Plan	28
3.	Theoretical Models of Translation	48
4.	Kinds of Research	58
5.	Questions, Claims, Hypotheses	69
6.	Relations between Variables	83
7.	Selecting and Analyzing Data	90
8.	Writing Your Research Report	101
9.	Presenting Your Research Orally	116
10.	Assessing Your Research	122
References		129
Index		140

Acknowledgements

The authors are deeply indebted to the following colleagues in Translation Studies who gave generously of their time and expertise in reading and commenting on the first draft of the **The Map**:

Gunilla Anderman, University of Surrey, England
Lynne Bowker, University of Ottawa, Canada
Michèle Cooke, University of Vienna, Austria
Margaret Gibbon, Dublin City University, Ireland
Daniel Gile, Université Lumière Lyon 2, France
Ritva Leppihalme, University of Helsinki, Finland 芬兰
Eithne O'Connell, Dublin City University, Ireland
Maeve Olohan, UMIST, England
Margaret Rogers, University of Surrey, England
Þebnem Susam-Sarajeva, University of Helsinki, Finland
Anne Tucker, SILD Division, European Parliament, Luxembourg.

We are also grateful to Translation Studies students at the University of Helsinki and Dublin City University for the feedback they provided on earlier versions of this book.

In addition, Jenny Williams would like to thank Dublin City University for granting her an Albert College Senior Fellowship (2001-2002), which enabled her to take research leave during the final stage of work on **The Map**.

Introduction

This book is intended as a guide for students who are required to undertake research in Translation Studies and present it in written and/or oral form. It is not an introduction to Translation Studies as such; we assume that readers already have a basic familiarity with the field. **The Map** aims to provide a step-by-step introduction to *doing research* in an area which, because of its interdisciplinary nature, can present the inexperienced researcher with a bewildering array of topics and methodologies. We have called it **The Map** because it is designed to help you find your way through a relatively new and uncharted terrain.

The point in an academic career at which a student engages in Translation Studies research for the first time varies from country to country. As an introductory text, **The Map** is addressed primarily to advanced BA students, to MA/MSc/MPhil students – whether on taught or research Masters programmes – as well as to PhD students who have had little previous experience of research in Translation Studies. We use these academic qualifications in the knowledge that they are culture-specific and with the intention only of indicating general levels of achievement.

Let us assume that a translation is a text in one language which is produced on the basis of a text in another language for a particular purpose. In the context of **The Map,** 'Translation Studies' is defined as the field of study devoted to describing, analyzing and theorizing the processes, contexts and products of the act of translation as well as the (roles of the) agents involved. In Chapter 1 we discuss research in Translation Studies under the following headings: Text Analysis and Translation, Translation Quality Assessment, Genre Translation, Multimedia Translation, Translation and Technology, Translation History, Translation Ethics, Terminology and Glossaries, Interpreting, the Translation Process, Translator Training and the Translation Profession.

We define research broadly as a "systematic investigation towards increasing the sum of knowledge" (Chambers 1989:845). We agree with Gillham (2000a: 2) that "research is about creating new knowledge, whatever the disciplines". Innovation is vital if a discipline is to grow and prosper. However, the definition of 'new knowledge' will vary according to the level at which the research is undertaken. An essay at advanced BA level will clearly differ in scope from a doctoral dissertation. 'Creating new knowledge' can consist in summarizing new research in an emerging field or providing a very small amount of new evidence to support or disconfirm an existing hypothesis at one end of the scale, to developing a new methodology for Translation History at the other.

The aim of Translation Studies research is therefore to make a contribution to the field which increases the sum of our knowledge. You can make your contribution in a number of ways:

- By providing new data;
- By suggesting an answer to a specific question;
- By testing or refining an existing hypothesis, theory or methodology;
- By proposing a new idea, hypothesis, theory or methodology.

Before you embark on research it is essential that you have some practical experience of translating, whether in the translation classroom or in a professional setting. A researcher in Translation Studies with no experience of translating is rather like the stereotypical backseat driver who, as we know, ends up being not only unpopular but also ignored and thus ineffectual – and sometimes even gets ejected from the vehicle! It is difficult, if not impossible, to appreciate the thought processes, choices, constraints and mechanisms involved in translation if you have never engaged in the process yourself. Theory and practice are as inseparable in Translation Studies as they are in all other fields of human endeavour. The mutual suspicion and hostility which used to exist between the translation profession and the Translation Studies research community has been giving way in recent times to a more productive relationship. The action research model recently proposed by Hatim (2001) offers some solutions to overcoming this unhelpful division. (See also Chesterman and Wagner 2002.)

Whether your desire to undertake research in Translation Studies is determined by a natural curiosity, a need to obtain a further qualification or a general desire for personal development, one of the first steps you will need to take is to identify a general area which interests you. Personal interest in and enthusiasm for your subject are vital if you want to make a success of it.

You might be interested in increasing our general understanding of translation or in improving some aspect of translation practice. The first kind of investigation might lead to better theories, better ways of looking at translation. The second would aim at improving translation quality or perhaps raising the status of translators themselves. Applied research of this kind can offer guidelines for better practice based on the study of successful professional translation. It can also test and perhaps revise prescriptive claims in the light of evidence from competent professional practice.

The initial idea for a research project can come from a very wide variety of sources, both academic and non-academic. You might be inspired by a book or a lecture on some aspect of Translation Studies, or by the work of a fellow student. You might be reading *Harry Potter* and wonder how it could be translated into Chinese. Or you could be trying to assemble your new flatpack bookcase and wonder how the largely incomprehensible instructions were produced. Or you could be playing your new video game and wondering who translated the original Japanese soundtrack into English. Or you could simply wake up one morning and wonder how all those European Union directives on Bovine Spongiform Encephalopathy got translated into the languages of the member states – or, indeed, ponder the implications of the enlargement of the European Union for translation.

The initial idea is exciting – but perhaps someone has already researched it? Or perhaps it's not feasible? Or perhaps it's not worth researching? To answer these questions you need to ascertain the current state of research in the field.

There are two reasons why this is essential:

1. The purpose of research is to *add* to the sum of knowledge; reinventing the wheel is a waste of everyone's time.
2. Your research is not taking place in a vacuum: it relates to what has gone before. Even if you consider that everything written on your topic to date is rubbish you must be able to substantiate this opinion and justify your own approach.

Research in Translation Studies can only grow and prosper if hypotheses are constantly being refined, developed and built upon, if ideas are constantly scrutinized. This is why you must first establish the current state of research on the topic you want to investigate.

Whether you have an initial idea or not, the standard Translation Studies reference works such as the annual *Bibliography of Translation Studies* (Bowker *et al.* 1998; 1999 and 2000a), the biannual *Translation Studies Abstracts* (Olohan 1998-), the *Dictionary of Translation Studies* (Shuttleworth and Cowie 1997), the *Encyclopedia of Literary Translation into English* (Classe 2000) and the *Routledge Encyclopedia of Translation Studies* (Baker 1998) all provide a good starting point. Recent surveys of the field include Chesterman (1997) and Munday (2001).

Chapter 1 of **The Map** gives an overview of twelve research areas in Translation Studies which will help you to identify a topic and establish some of the current research questions relating to it. Chapter 2 will assist you in planning your research project: time spent drawing up your research plan is time well spent and can save you time and trouble in the long run. Chapters 3 to 7 provide some of the conceptual and methodological tools you will need. Chapters 8 and 9 are about how to present your research; and, finally, chapter 10 deals with some of the criteria which you and others will use to assess your research.

The Map will thus take you through the research process, which can be described as consisting of a number of stages, some of which will overlap:

> ➤ choosing an area
> ➤ making a preliminary plan
> ➤ searching through the literature
> ➤ reading and thinking
> ➤ defining the research question
> ➤ revising the plan
> ➤ collecting data
> ➤ analyzing the data
> ➤ processing the results
> ➤ writing a draft
> ➤ evaluating, eliciting feedback
> ➤ thinking of implications

> ➤ finalizing the text
> ➤ presenting your research report.

How you use **The Map** will depend on your current position and your destination. If you are at the beginning of your journey into research in Translation Studies, we suggest you read this book chronologically. If you are about to give an oral presentation, you might skip to Chapter 9. Students in the throes of writing up their research might find Chapter 8 particularly useful. If you are nearing completion of your project, the checklist in Chapter 10 might be the best place to start.

1. Areas in Translation Research

This chapter gives an overview of 12 research areas in Translation Studies. The list itself is by no means exhaustive nor is the coverage of each topic comprehensive. It is merely intended to provide a point of orientation – a **Map** – for researchers setting out to explore Translation Studies.

1.1 Text Analysis and Translation

Source Text Analysis

Source text analysis focuses on the analysis of the source text itself, examining the various aspects of it that might give rise to translation problems. This has an obvious relevance in translator training. A good primary background reference is Nord (1991). The point of such an analysis is to prepare for a translation: after a careful analysis of the syntactic, semantic and stylistic features of the source text, it will presumably be easier to come up with adequate translation solutions. This kind of focus is usually linked to an analysis of the communicative situation of the translation itself: who it will be for, what its function is intended to be, and so on.

Comparison of Translations and their Source Texts

The *analysis of translated texts* involves the textual comparison of a translation with its original. A *translation comparison* deals with several translations, into the same language or into different languages, of the same original. Such topics cannot deal with every possible aspect of the texts, of course, so you have to choose the aspect(s) you want to focus on. You might take a particular aspect of the source text, such as a particular stylistic or syntactic feature, and examine the corresponding sections in the translations. Or you could start with a kind of translation problem (the translation of passive sentences, or dialect, or allusions, for instance), and see how your translator(s) have solved the problem, what *translation strategies* they have used. Or you could start with a kind of translation strategy, some kind of change or shift between source and target texts (e.g. the strategy of explicitation), and examine its conditions of use. (For references to research on explicitation, see e.g. the entry for it in Shuttleworth and Cowie 1997.) In all these cases, your aim would be to discover patterns of correspondence between the texts. In other words, you would be interested in possible regularities of the translator's behaviour, and maybe also in the general principles that seem to determine how certain things get translated under certain conditions. (See Leuven-Zwart 1989 and 1990 for a methodology for translation analysis.)

Comparison of Translations and Non-translated Texts

This kind of analysis compares translations into a given language with similar texts originally written in that language. Traditionally in Translation Studies scholars have referred to these as *parallel texts*; with the advent of corpus-based Translation Studies these original-language texts are now sometimes called *comparable texts*. The idea here is to examine the way in which translations tend to differ from other texts in the target language, the way they often turn out to be not quite natural. (This might, or might not, be a good thing – depending on the aim and type of the translation in question.) This kind of research is quantitative, and usually deals with relative differences of distribution of particular textual features. For some examples, see several of the papers in Olohan (2000) and the special issue of *Meta* 43(4) (1998).

All the above research areas involve forms of contrastive text analysis and contrastive stylistics. They thus depend implicitly on some kind of contrastive theory. (See Chesterman 1998 for the relation between the theories and methodologies of contrastive analysis and Translation Studies.)

Translation with Commentary

A *translation with commentary* (or *annotated translation*) is a form of introspective and retrospective research where you yourself translate a text and, at the same time, write a commentary on your own translation process. This commentary will include some discussion of the translation assignment, an analysis of aspects of the source text, and a reasoned justification of the kinds of solutions you arrived at for particular kinds of translation problems. One value of such research lies in the contribution that increased self-awareness

can make to translation quality. You might also want to show
whether you have found any helpful guidelines for your translation
decisions in what you have read in Translation Studies. A classical
example of such a commentary is Bly (1984), where the translator
describes in detail the various stages he went through during the
translation of a poem.

1.2 Translation Quality Assessment

Translation quality assessment, unlike most of the areas mentioned
here, is overtly evaluative. Translations are assessed in real life in
several circumstances: during training, in examinations for official
certification, by critics and reviewers, and ultimately of course by
the ordinary reader. Some assessment methods have been developed by scholars, others by teachers, and still others by the
translation industry. Some international standards have been set up
in order to control or assure quality (ISO 9002, DIN 2345).

We can distinguish three general approaches to quality assessment. One is *source-oriented*, based on the relation between the
translation and its source text. Assessment methods of this kind set
up definitions of required equivalence and then classify various kinds
of deviance from this equivalence. (See e.g. House 1997 and
Schäffner 1998; the special issues of *TTR* 2(2) 1989, *The Translator* 6(2) 2000 and *Meta* 46(2) 2001.)

The second approach is *target-language oriented*. Here, the
relation at stake is not with the source text but with the target
language. Equivalence is not a central concept here. This approach
uses text analysis (see above) in order to assess the differences
between the translation in question and other comparable texts in
the target language. The idea is to measure the translation's degree
of naturalness – on the assumption that this is often a feature to be
desired. (See Toury 1995 and Leuven-Zwart 1989 and 1990.)

The third approach has to do with the assessment of *translation
effects* – on clients, teachers, critics and readers. In the case of a
literary translation, you might examine published reviews in the
press. (See e.g. Maier 1998 and Fawcett 2000.) Or you might interview publishers or readers about their expectations concerning
translation quality. Or you might carry out comprehension tests on

the translation, to see how well people understood it. Or you might send out a questionnaire to translation teachers, to see what kinds of marking methods and criteria they used. This approach finds functional and/or communicative theories of translation useful, such as skopos theory, since the skopos is the 'purpose for which a translator designs a translation ("translatum") in agreement with his commissioner' (Vermeer 1996: 7).

All three general approaches are illustrated in chapter 5 of Chesterman (1997).

1.3 Genre Translation

By 'genre' we mean both traditional literary genres such as drama, poetry and prose fiction as well as other well established and clearly defined types of text for translation such as multimedia texts, religious texts, children's literature, tourism texts, technical texts and legal documents. See Swales (1991) and Trosborg (1997) for an overview of definitions and methodological concepts.

For a good introduction to the major issues in literary translation, see Bassnett (1991), Gaddis Rose (1997), Bassnett and Lefevere (1998) and Boase-Beier and Holman (1999).

Drama

The status of drama texts is a major issue here, and among the first questions to be addressed are: is this play being translated to be performed or to be read? If it is to be performed, what sort of translation is required – a rough one which will be a starting point for the production or a fully performable one or something in between? The process of translation 'from page to stage' throws up many research questions – for example, the role(s) of the various participants: translator, director, actors. There is plenty of scope for undertaking a case study of an individual production, researching the biography of an established drama translator, comparing different translations of the same play.

Other topics which suggest themselves include the question of (trans)location: (where) is the foreign play located in the target culture? Brecht has been located in the north-east of England and Chekov in the west of Ireland: what are the reasons for / implications of such (trans)locations? See Upton (2000) for a discussion of cultural relocation. Performability – which ranges from body language to choice of props – is another worthwhile topic.

See Johnston (1996) for a range of views from translators for the stage, Aaltonen (1996), Anderman (1998) and Bassnett (2000) for further reading.

Poetry

Poetic texts can provide interesting material for translation research, especially if time is limited, since the texts concerned can be quite short. Here the major topics include

- The aim of the translation – a prose version or a poem?
- The translation of metre, cadence, rhythm, rhyme
- The profile of the translator – can only poets translate poetry?
- How do translators translate poetry?

See Holmes (1994) for an overview of the issues in poetry translation and both De Beaugrande (1978) and Bly (1984) for a 'step by step' guide to translating a poem.

Prose Fiction

This is the field where most full-time literary translators earn their living. As it is impossible to research the totality of a novel, or even a short story, it is important to select one aspect. This could be the narrative perspective of the author/translator, the translation of dialogue, the handling of culture-specific items or the translation of humour. Sometimes it can make sense to concentrate on the first chapter or opening scene, since this often sets the tone for the remainder of the work.

One under-researched area here is contemporary translators themselves: their biographies, how they obtain translation contracts, their relations with editors and publishers. It could be interesting to interview a translator and discover how they go about their work, whether they write prefaces / afterwords, whether they use footnotes or provide glossaries (see Pelegrin 1987).

A further area worth investigating is the reception of translated works: how do critics review translated works? What do they have to say about translation (if anything)? See Fawcett (2000) for a study of the reception of translation in the quality press.

Bassnett (1998) provides a useful categorization of the types of research which can be undertaken at doctoral level in literary translation.

Religious Texts

In order to engage in translation criticism, you will need in-depth knowledge of one (or more) of the source languages. Major research questions concerning religious texts have to do with

- The enormous temporal and cultural gap between the societies for which these texts were written and the societies for which they have been translated
- The tension between treating religious texts such as the Bible as a sacred text in which every word is holy (which requires a word-for-word translation) and using it as a missionizing text (which requires a target-culture-centred approach). See Nida (1964) and Nida and Taber (1969).

Gaddis Rose (2000) and Jasper (1993) provide useful starting points to what is, potentially, a vast field.

A different approach would be to compare different translations of a particular sacred text (e.g. the Koran) into one language, either diachronically or synchronically (see Lewis 1981). Here, again, it would be important to focus on a particular aspect. For an overview of currently available English translations of the Bible, see Gregory (2001).

In European societies the Reformation was a crucial and dangerous time for Bible translators, and the writings of Wycliffe, Tyndale, Luther, Calvin and others provide material for research questions such as: how did these translators go about their work? Why did they engage in such a dangerous activity? (See Lefevere 1992.)

One side-aspect of Bible translation which has been frequently commented on but little researched is the influence of the 1611 King James Bible (the *Authorized Version*) on the development of the English language: is it true that anyone translating out of English needs to be familiar with this text? And if so: in what circumstances? And with what aspect(s)? (See Biblia 1997.)

Children's Literature

Definition is important and difficult here. Are you dealing with literature (designed to be) read *by* children or *to* children? What age group(s) do you mean? Does 'literature' include only books or could it also include TV programmes, films and software? Children's literature spans many genres – from poems and fairytales to fiction and scientific writing. It is also expected to fulfil a number of different functions, e.g. entertainment, socialization, language development as well as general education.

Although Klingberg's (1986) rather prescriptive approach has been replaced in recent years by a more descriptive one (Oittinen 1993; Puurtinen 1995), his list of five potential research areas (1986:9) still constitutes a good starting point for the researcher.

Tourism Texts

The travel, tourism and heritage sectors, which involve a high degree of cross-cultural and linguistic contact, have grown exponentially over the last forty years and have taken on enormous economic importance in many countries throughout the world. It is therefore striking how little attention has been paid to the texts that make this possible. There is enormous scope here for different kinds of research: what is the current provision of translated material in a particular locality? How does this match the needs of the sector? What kinds of strategies are appropriate in the translation of materials for tourists?

Snell-Hornby (1989) discusses some practical examples of translating tourism texts and Kelly (2000) situates tourism texts in the context of translator training. Cronin (2000) offers a more philosophical view.

Technical Texts

Technical translation covers the translation of many kinds of specialized texts in science and technology, and also in other disciplines such as economics and medicine. In the business sector, this work is often referred to as multilingual documentation. The translation of these texts needs a high level of subject knowledge, and a mastery of the relevant terminology. Some research topics concern problems of style and clarity, text-type conventions, culture-specific reader expectations and the special problems of particular document types such as patents. Applied research in this field also works on improving the training of technical translators. Other research looks more widely at the historical role of translators in the dissemination of knowledge. For an introductory survey, see Wright and Wright (1993). Pearson (1999) and Bowker (2000b) give illustrations of corpus-based approaches to research in this area.

Legal Texts

Legal translation has evolved into a sub-field in its own right, specializing in the translation problems and norms of this text type. An illustrative issue is the question of how creative the legal translator can be, and under what circumstances. Another is the role of the translator as co-drafter of the original. See Morris (1995), Gémar (1995) and Šarčević (1997).

1.4 Multimedia Translation

Audiovisual texts are primarily spoken texts – radio/TV programmes, films, DVDs, videos, opera, theatre – which are translated either by revoicing or sur-/subtitling (Luyken 1991). Revoicing replaces the original spoken text with a translation in the target language; sur-/subtitling leaves the original spoken or sung text intact and adds a written translation on screen. The choice of translation procedure depends on a variety of factors – and is itself a topic for research: see O'Connell (1998) for an overview.

Revoicing

Revoicing includes voice-over, narration, free commentary and lip-sync dubbing. Major research questions include:

- Which type of revoicing is appropriate in which circumstances?
- Which type of synchrony should have precedence in particular circumstances? (see Fodor 1976; Whitman-Linsen 1992)
- Case studies of revoiced material (e.g. Herbst 1994)
- What role does the translator play in the revoicing process?

Sur-/subtitling

Ivarsson (1992) provides a good overview of a field where research deals with:

- The technical constraints of sur-/subtitling
- The training of sur-/subtitlers (see also Gambier 1998)
- Analyses of sur-/subtitled material
- Subtitling as a language learning / teaching tool (see Vanderplank 1999)
- Subtitling for the deaf and hard-of-hearing (e.g. De Linde and Kay 1999).

Common to both areas of audiovisual translation is an interest in audiovisual translation in a minority language context: see O'Connell (1994).

Gambier and Gottlieb (2001) provide an introduction to the whole emerging field of Multimedia Translation.

1.5 Translation and Technology

While technology has become an integral part of the translation profession, there has been little, if any, research into many aspects of the technology itself. There is a range of topics to be investigated here:

Evaluating Software

Language Engineering is producing more and more software for Machine Translation and Computer-Aided Translation, such as terminology management programs and translation memory systems which enable translators to access previous translations and similar documents. The evaluation of this software can take the form of a small-scale or large-scale research project. Evaluation can be quite complicated, and you need to establish clearly formulated criteria – see Arnold *et al.* (1994) for some suggestions. You could, for example, use an existing MT package, such as *Telegraph*, to translate a number of texts of a particular text type and draw conclusions about the strengths and weaknesses of the software or make recommendations for improvements. Alternatively, you could compare two or more products which are designed to do the same thing, such as MT systems or translation memory systems. Another type of software which has not yet been researched is the translation facility on Personal Digital Assistants and other mobile computing devices.

Software Localization

Software localization is the process which adapts a software product for a target language and culture. This includes adapting the interface, online help files as well as the accompanying documentation. A workplace study, tracking, for example, a localization project from commissioning to delivery, could investigate the role of the participants in the process – from project manager through in-house/ freelance translator to software engineer. Mechanisms of quality control are another worthwhile research topic. Or you might evaluate the finished product. Esselink (2000) and Hall and Hudson (1997) provide a good introduction to the field.

Effects of Technology

Although Translation Memory systems are now widely used, there is relatively little research on the impact they have either on the way translators work or on translation output. Kenny (1999) and Bowker (2002) contain discussions of the effects of technology on the translation process. Using a questionnaire you could establish the attitudes of translators to this type of software; or you could obtain permission from a translation company to analyze aspects of texts translated in this way (see Merkel 1998 for an example of a study on consistency).

Website Translation

Here you could:

- establish the current practice in website translation
- investigate the effect of website constraints and user demands on translators' decisions at both the micro and macro levels
- evaluate the product
- explore the feasibility of using controlled languages in website design to facilitate translation.

Cheng (2000) provides a case study of website translation.

The Place of Technology in Translator Training

As early as 1996 Schäler made a plea for the introduction of Translation Technology into every translator training programme (Schäler 1998). Kiraly (2000: 123-139) outlines how this could be done, both practically and methodologically. You could establish to what extent this has happened in your country. By use of questionnaires and interviews you could also investigate how this could be done better: what sort of technological skills would be most appropriate in which contexts? Who should design and teach such courses? See Austermühl (2001) for a clear explanation of the software products, information resources and online services now available to trainee and professional translators. (See also the section on Corpus-based Translation Studies in 4.5 below.)

1.6 Translation History

Translations can have long-term effects on whole languages and cultures, of course, and these too can be assessed in a historical or cultural study. If this is your field of interest, you would need a rather different theoretical apparatus, such as you will find in culture studies, norm theory or polysystem theory (see the relevant entries in Shuttleworth and Cowie 1997 for an introduction).

Chesterman (1989), Lefevere (1992) and Robinson (1997a) provide good introductions to Translation History, and Pym's *Method in Translation History* (1998) is an indispensable guide to undertaking research in this field. The Literary Translation Project at the University of Göttingen, which was funded over a number of years by the Deutsche Forschungsgemeinschaft, has also published an impressive body of research under the 'Göttinger Beiträge zur Internationalen Übersetzungsforschung' rubric, which has made a major contribution to our knowledge and understanding of translation history.

The major research questions in Translation History are to do with: Who? What? Why? and How?

Who?

In recent years Translation Studies has been focusing increasingly on translators themselves: their backgrounds, their relations with publishers and editors, their motivation and their translation practice (see Delisle and Woodsworth 1995 and Delisle 1999). There is considerable scope for 'excavation' here in discovering forgotten translators and placing their translations in the context of their lives and work as well as the context of the intercultural space they inhabit between two languages and cultures.

What?

A fascinating area of research investigates which texts are translated (or not translated) in particular cultures at particular times. How, for example, did the social and political upheavals in eastern Europe in the early 1990s affect the volume and nature of translations into Polish, Slovak, Czech, Russian and so on? Translation can also shed light on relations between majority and minority language communities, between imperial centres and colonial fringes as well as between victors and vanquished. Research into reviews of translated works can give insights into their reception and the reasons for their success or lack of it.

Why?

One of the major questions in Translation History concerns the reason(s) why particular texts are translated at particular times. Reasons can range from the use of translation to establish a national literature, a particular set of relations between the two cultures concerned or the individual interests of a particular publisher. A good illustration of this type of research is Kohlmeyer's (1994) work on the popularity of Oscar Wilde's plays on the German stage during the Nazi period.

How?

Translators' strategies through the ages have varied enormously, depending on the demands of commissioners, publishers, readers as well as their own personal preferences. Studies which undertake detailed analyses of individual translations in their social and historical context have an important role to play in filling in the gaps in translation history. Research questions here attempt to link the micro (i.e. textual) and macro (i.e. social/historical/intercultural) aspects of Translation History.

Cronin (1996) provides a good illustration of a study which investigates the role of translation in the political, linguistic and literary
history of one country. See Part II of the *Routledge Encyclopedia*
(Baker 1998) for useful surveys of Translation History.

1.7 Translation Ethics

Much of the older work in translation theory was prescriptive: it
made claims about what a translator should do, and thus sought to
establish guidelines for 'good' translations. Opinions naturally varied... Contemporary work has problematized the concept of 'good'
translating in many ways, and brought new dimensions to our understanding of translation ethics, although many problems remain,
both conceptual and practical.

Different kinds of ethics
How could we best reconcile the ethical conclusions represented
by different approaches, different kinds of ethics? Some arguments
are based on the value of a true or faithful representation of the
original, of the Other. Others start from the idea that translating is a
form of service for a client, and thus value loyalty. Others again
take understanding or cooperation as the primary values to be served.
Still others propose an ethics based on norms and the value of trust.
Research focusing on these questions involves conceptual analysis,
and is often influenced by debates in moral philosophy.

Cultural and ideological factors
Another set of questions has been raised by the cultural turn in Translation Studies: this has led scholars to look at how translations have
been influenced by cultural and ideological factors, and how translations in turn have effects on target readers and cultures. These
effects can have huge ethical dimensions. Keywords here are

- power, emancipation (see Robinson 1997b)
- gender (see Von Flotow 1997)
- post-colonialism, nationalism, hegemony (see Bassnett and
  Trivedi 1999)
- minority, cultural identity (see Venuti 1998)
- the translator's visibility (see Venuti 1995a).

Translations have been, and still are, powerful instruments in ideological programmes. An analysis of these topics brings to the surface major sociopolitical issues, which are themselves ultimately based on aims that can be subjected to an ethical analysis. Research is usually historical in nature, often focusing on a case study. (For a survey of this kind of work, see Robinson 1997b.)

Codes of Practice

At a more practical level, many national professional associations of translators have an official code of good practice which states the ethical principles that professional translators are expected to abide by. These codes are attempts to translate abstract ideas and values into concrete form, and also to meet the needs of translation as a business activity, involving e.g. the requirement of professional secrecy. It is interesting to compare the codes used in different countries. Some countries even have professional oaths that must be sworn as part of the accreditation process. (See 1.12 below.)

There are also internationally agreed documents concerning ethical translatorial behaviour. One is the Translator's Charter, and another is the Nairobi Declaration. For both, see the homepage of FIT (Fédération Internationale des Traducteurs) at <http://fit-ift.org>. These are worth analyzing and comparing. They set out principles governing not only how translators should behave (translators' obligations), but also how society should behave towards translators (translators' rights). One important issue touched on is that of translator's copyright: translations are forms of intellectual property, and their creators should thus have rights over this property. (See e.g. Venuti 1995b.) However, the legal position of translators varies rather widely from country to country in this respect. What might be done to improve translators' rights? See Phelan (2001) for Codes of Ethics from Interpreters' Organizations.

Personal vs. Professional Ethics

Other recurrent topics in translation ethics have to do with the borderline between professional and personal ethics; what to do when loyalties to author and reader clash; the translator's right or duty to improve originals; the boundaries of a translator's responsibility; how postmodernism has brought new ideas into the debate about translation ethics; and when it might be more ethical not to translate at all.

Most of this research is either conceptual or historical in nature, looking at translation ethics descriptively (what are the ethical values given highest priority by different parties? how do they vary?). However, some scholars of translation ethics wish not just to describe and understand the world of translation, but also to change it. Their approach is thus prescriptive in intent.

Further reading: Pym (1997), Koskinen (2000), and the special issue of *The Translator* 7(2) 2001.

1.8 Terminology and Glossaries

Research in terminology serves both theoretical and practical goals. The methodology is basically one of detailed conceptual analysis, but it also involves bibliographical fieldwork and corpus processing. You first need to know the basics of terminology theory and its origins in the growing need for international standardization during the past century. This means e.g. understanding the difference between general language and domain-restricted language (e.g. Melby 1995), and knowing how to define a 'term'. You also need to master the methodological and technical skills required: learning how to formulate a valid definition; learning how to represent various kinds of conceptual systems based on different kinds of relationships between concepts (e.g. hierarchical concept diagrams of various kinds); and learning how to use the computer programs such as Trados MultiTerm that have been developed specifically for terminological work.

In the area of theory, cognitive and philosophical questions come to mind: what is a concept? What do terms represent? How do non-linguistic signs relate to linguistic signs? How can synonymy be accommodated in current models? How can current models be more dynamic? How do terms evolve? How do terms cross language boundaries? What is the relationship between terminology and knowledge engineering? What types of relation can be established between concepts beyond abstract (genus-species) and part-whole relations and how are these realized cross-linguistically? What can prototype theory tell us about the classification of terms and concepts?

What can an experiential epistemological approach tell us about terms and their meanings? How can equivalence be defined at a text rather than a system level? See the journals *Terminology* and *Terminology, Science and Research* for an overview of the major theoretical issues, as well as the publications in the Information Infrastructure Task Force (IITF) series published by TermNet.

In practical research you choose a domain and a language or two, and begin with documentary searches and corpus work: this is term indentification and extraction. Some computer programs exist which can help in the automatic extraction of terms, and more are being developed. Then, via parallel conceptual analysis and definition comparison, you can gradually compile the terminology database for the domain and languages you have chosen. The work might eventually involve term harmonization and language planning. At advanced BA/MA level, the domain will be very restricted (glassblowing, basketball,...). See Wright and Budin (1997 and 2001), Cabré (1999) and Sager (1990). See Pearson (1998) for an introduction to corpus-based approaches.

Additional specialist journals in this area include *Terminologie et Traduction, La Banque des Mots, Terminolies Nouvelles.* Also worth consulting are the relevant international standards: ISO/DIS 1087-1.2 *Terminology work – Vocabulary – Part 1. Theory and application, 1999.*

1.9 Interpreting

Interpreting research has developed rapidly from earlier anecdotal reports to systematic work exploring linguistic, communicative, cognitive and socio-cultural aspects of interpreting. The general field of interpreting can be analyzed in different ways. One distinction concerns the mode of interpreting: simultaneous or consecutive. Another classification concerns the social situation where interpreting is needed, such as:

- Conference interpreting (usually simultaneous, in one direction)
- Liason interpreting, also known as dialogue or community interpreting (usually bi-directional)
- Court interpreting (usually bi-directional).

Research on interpreting usually focuses on one of these types. Useful surveys are to be found in the special issues of *Target* 7(1) 1995, *The Translator* 5(2) 1999, as well as in Carr *et al.* (1996), Gambier *et al.* (1997), Wadensjö (1998), Englund and Hyltenstam (2000), Mason (2000 and 2001) and Gile et al. (2001). See also the journals *Interpreting* and *Meta*, and the *Interpreting Studies Reader* edited by Shlesinger and Pöchhacker (2001).

Sample research topics can be grouped under the following headings:

Cognitive Studies
*   Neurophysiological studies of the interpreter's brain in action (not for beginners!)
*   The functioning of memory in simultaneous interpreting
*   The effect of time-lag on the final quality of the interpretation (in simultaneous)

Behavioural Studies
*   The note-taking techniques used in consecutive interpreting
*   Studies of the strategies interpreters use to prepare for a task
*   Studies of how interpreters cope with particular problems such as a speaker's unusual form of delivery, unusual time constraints, unusual stress conditions
*   Time-sharing in dialogue interpreting (between the various speakers)
*   Eye-contact between the interpreter and the other participants

Linguistic Studies
*   Language-pair-specific studies of how interpreters tend to render various kinds of structures under certain conditions
*   Studies of what and when interpreters tend to omit or condense
*   Style shifts during interpreting: do interpreters tend to gravitate towards a neutral style, even when their speakers are using a more formal or informal register?

Sociological Studies, Ethics, History
*   The negotiation of power and politeness relations among the participants in a dialogue interpreting situation;

- The ethical responsibility of the interpreter, whose side is he/she on?
- The history of interpreting.

Interpreter Training
- Comparative studies of professional and trainee interpreters working under similar conditions; or of 'naïve', untrained interpreters
- Comparative studies of how interpreters are trained in different institutions.

Quality Assessment
- Studies of the reactions of hearers to various aspects of interpreting quality: intonation, voice quality, speed, pauses, grammatical errors, etc.
- Experiments with various methods of assessing the quality of interpreting.

Special Kinds of Interpreting
- The special requirements of court interpreting
- Interpreting for the deaf; sign-language interpreting
- Interpreting for the blind: e.g. the simultaneous oral narration of films (setting, action and script...)
- The use of whispered interpreting (*chuchotage*).

The gathering of empirical data in interpreting research can take a good deal of time and effort. You may need video-recordings as well as tapes. Transcribing a tape-recording is extremely time-consuming. Corpora of recorded and/or transcribed material are therefore extremely valuable as research tools also for other scholars.

1.10 The Translation Process

Workplace Studies
Under this heading we group a few forms of research that have to do with the working lives and conditions of professional translators. They represent ways of studying the sociology of translation.

One such approach is to observe a given translator or translators during a defined period in their everyday work, perhaps combining this research method with interviews. You might be interested in the translators' working procedures: how they distribute their time between different tasks, how they use reference material or parallel texts, whom they contact when they get stuck, how much coffee they consume... When and how do they revise their text? How do they keep up to date with the latest ideas and developments? What use do they make of computer aids, translation memory programs, the Internet? Do literary translators work differently from translators of other kinds of texts? (See Mossop 2000 for further suggestions.)

An important value of this research is that it allows us to formulate and test hypotheses about how translators behave, but it also has obvious relevance for translator training. Do professional translators actually follow the advice that teachers traditionally give them – e.g. about reading the source text through first? How could we best incorporate information about real translators' working lives into a training programme? What do professional translators think about their own earlier training (questionnaire...)?

Research of this kind at the institutional level broadens the focus to include the translation procedures and policies of companies, agencies, cities, etc. How do official bodies of various kinds organize their own translation practices? What policies do they have for meeting their multilingual communication needs? How have they analyzed these needs in the first place? What use do they make of in-house or freelance staff? What kinds of quality control systems do they use? Do they actually talk about translation at all, or prefer to speak of multilingual documentation? Research here would probably involve a combination of observation, interviews and questionnaires. (See e.g. Lambert 1996.)

One extension of this approach is research on best practice. This involves studying the working processes of translators (or multilingual documentation specialists...) and attempting to correlate these processes with translation quality. Which kinds of working methods seem to lead to the best quality results? To carry out such research, you would obviously need to establish both a way of analyzing working procedures and a way of measuring quality. Very little systematic research has been done on this topic so far. (See, however, Sprung 2000.)

Another line of research focuses on the analysis of what translators themselves say or write about their work. The material here includes translators' prefaces and afterwords, their footnotes, personal essays and memoirs of translators, interviews with translators, TV programmes about translators or interpreters, and so on. What do translators think about their work, and about themselves as translators? What kind of role model do they seem to have in their minds? How do their attitudes correlate with their particular working conditions, or with the quality of their work? Whom do they especially admire? This kind of research obviously contributes to the status of translators as people worth studying, and hence enhances their social visibility. This in turn might influence what other people in society think about translators, and hence the discourse on translation in general – i.e. what people say and think about translation.

Protocol Studies

This research seeks to investigate the translator's internal decision-making process, by using think-aloud methods or retrospective interviews. Think-aloud protocols can also be linked to computer records of key-stroke usage, so that you can study the translator's use of time in detail. Where do the pauses and hesitations come, the corrections and alterations? (See Kussmaul and Tirkkonen-Condit 1995; Tirkkonen-Condit and Jääskeläinen 2000; Hansen 1999 and also 4.3 below.)

1.11 Translator Training

The research questions in Translator Training revolve around four main areas:

Curriculum Design

This relates to the content of translator-training programmes: which elements are essential/desirable in (which) translator-training programmes and why? What is the relative importance (in which context?) of training mother-tongue competence, subject-field knowledge, familiarity with translation software and so on? Another hotly debated topic is whether translator training should take place at undergraduate or postgraduate level. A comparative-descriptive study of practice in a number of different countries could shed light on universal as opposed to local, culture-specific aspects of Translator Training.

Implementation

Here we are dealing with the content, delivery and evaluation of particular components in a translator-training programme. For example, most programmes include at least one course in 'Specialized Translation'. Yet little agreement seems to exist on the degree of specialization appropriate at any particular level, the qualifications required in the teacher of such a course, appropriate classroom management techniques and/or the best way(s) to provide feedback to students on their work.

Research needs to be carried out on the role of Translation Technology in translator-training programmes as well as on the content of Translation Technology modules. For example, a Translation Technology module could include terminology management, translation memory system(s), website translation, software localization: which elements are most appropriate in which situations? How can such a course be delivered? In a lecture hall? In a computer lab? Online? (See also 1.5 above.)

Typical Problem Areas

Are there 'universal problems' which (almost) all trainees encounter? Possible candidates might be: improper use of (bilingual) dictionaries, inadequate textual competence in specific fields. (See Kussmaul 1995.) How could such problems be tackled? Residence in the country/ies of the Source and/or Target Language (how long? how structured?) is another research topic in this area.

Professional Dimension

How can trainees best be introduced to the profession in the course of their studies? Issues in this context range from participation in national Translators Associations through tendering for contracts and billing to questions of ethics. The (un)desirability of company placements is another issue here. As the translation profession is changing so rapidly, there is plenty of scope for up-to-date workplace studies on current practice – and the research questions allied to practice – in multilingual documentation companies.

Besides Kussmaul (1995), Kiraly (1995, 2000) and Schäffner and Adab (2000), most publications in translator training can be found in the Proceedings of major international conferences such as those organized by FIT (Fédération Internationale des Trad-ucteurs), EST (European Society for Translation Studies) as well as by Translator Training Schools (e.g. Dollerup and Appel 1996; Delisle and Lee-Jahnke 1998) and, occasionally, in special issues of journals.

Empirical data is abundant and largely unexplored in this topic area: curricula, syllabi, trainers, trainees, examination scripts and other forms of trainee assessment are accessible in many transla-tor-training institutions throughout the world.

1.12 The Translation Profession

This is quite a new area of research devoted to the professional context in which translators work. Here research can either be his-torical or contemporary. Historical research might look at how a professional association has developed in a country, region or con-tinent. Contemporary research could deal with issues relating to the current situation of the professional association(s) in your country. If there is more than one (or none), your research might investigate why this is so. Research questions in this area revolve around:

- Qualifications for membership/ membership categories
- The nature of the certification process (if one exists)
- The employment status of the members (freelance, salaried trans-lators in the private/public sector, part-time/full-time?) and their specialism (technical, literary etc.)
- The Association's code of ethics
- The benefits of membership
- The Association's role in translation policy development at local, regional or national level
- The Association's programme of professional development for members.

See the list of Translation Associations in Part IV of Hatim (2001), and also the journal *Babel*, for an introduction to this area.

2. From the Initial Idea to the Plan

The stage between deciding on a general area of research and drawing up your research plan is a crucial one. All the decisions you take now will have a significant influence on the implementation and ultimate success of your project.

The planning process consists of a number of phases, covered in this and the following five chapters, which take place more or less simultaneously. In this chapter we discuss some preliminary practical and methodological issues which you will need to consider as you work on your initial idea. Chapters 3 to 7 deal with some more theoretical aspects of methodology.

2.1 Refine the Initial Idea

When you have decided on a general area, one that you are genuinely, subjectively interested in, the next stage is to narrow it down to a plausible research topic that you can carry out in the time available to you, with the resources you have. Then ask yourself lots of questions about it, from different points of view: who, what, where, when ... Booth *et al.* (1995: 40) suggest the following kinds of questions:

- How could you divide your topic into parts? What are the relations between these parts? Also: what whole is your topic a part of? How is it related to more general topics?
- What is the history of your topic? What larger history is it a part of?
- What are the categories of your topic, its main concepts? What kind of variation does your topic show? How are different instances of it similar and different?
- What is the value of the topic in respect to its usefulness? Are some parts of it more valuable than other parts?

Then try to emphasize questions that begin with *how* and *why*. Which of these interests you most? Booth *et al.* (1995) suggest the following steps as you think about defining the main aim of your research:

Step 1: Name your general topic: I am working on translation history.

Step 2: Suggest a question: ... because I want to find out who translated the Grimms' fairy tales into English and how they did so.

Step 3: Motivate the question: ... in order to understand more about how translators relate to their texts in a specific historical context.

Step 1 says what you are interested in. Step 2 states what you don't know about it. Step 3 gives you the rationale for your research: it makes explicit the reason why you want to study X, why you want to know more about it. The link between 2 and 3 must be well motivated. You can check that your rationale is logical by working backwards: if anyone wanted to understand why/how/whether ... [3], they would need, for instance, to find out why/what/how/ ... [2]: right? How convincing did that feel? Is your rationale too general, or too specific?

The final step, which we could call Step 4, is what links a question that interests you to things that interest others, your readers, the rest of the scholarly community. This step relates your question to a problem that is significant to others – a practical problem, maybe, or a research problem. Or maybe you are discovering a new problem? In what we reformulate here as Step 4, you state your aim in terms of how you wish to affect the reader:

> Step 4. ... in fact, what I want to do is *show you* why/what/how/who ... (Step 2) ... in order to *explain to you* why/how ... (Step 3).

Ultimately, what you want to do is to change the way the reader thinks about something. (We will return to this in Chapter 8, on writing your research report.)

2.2 Talk to Someone who Knows

You may find it helpful to discuss your ideas as they evolve with someone who has experience in the area you want to research. This person may be the lecturer teaching your translation course, or, if you're fortunate enough to be in a Translation Studies Department, there will be a number of active researchers you can approach. While you may feel in awe of people whose names appear in journals and on book covers, they will – in most cases! – be delighted to talk to anyone interested in their work.

Face-to-face communication is by far the easiest way to discuss and develop ideas, exchange information and generally get a feel for the parameters of the area you are considering researching.

An alternative means of communication is, of course, email – which you may have to use if you are far away from Translation Studies researchers. While this can work very well in many cases, you need to bear in mind that colleagues can get inundated by emails and may take some time to answer yours. Email can also easily lead to misunderstandings: while it may be perfectly normal in your culture to address some one you don't know by their first name and begin your email with the equivalent of "I want …", this may not be acceptable in other cultures. In other words: observe basic email etiquette.

2.3 Check out other Resources

We have already mentioned the colleagues in Translation Studies. The other key people are the university/college librarians. Establishing a good relationship with the librarian(s) in your subject area as well as those in the Inter-Library loan section of your university / college library is essential for your research.

Next you should check out the Translation Studies journals. Start with the general ones such as *Across Languages and Cultures, Babel, Language International, Lebende Sprachen, Meta, Perspectives: Studies in Translatology, Target, The Translator, TTR*. Usually it's sufficient to look at the last five years to get an idea of the general trends in the field. As your field of inquiry narrows, you can then move on to more specialized journals such as – depending on your interests – *International Journal of Corpus Linguistics, International Journal of Lexicography, Interpreting, Languages in Contrast, Machine Translation, Terminology. From* here your search will lead you to the standard work in the field.

Your national Translators' Association is a valuable resource available to you. It will most likely have a journal or newsletter: subscribe to it! The Association may organize workshops and seminars on many aspects of translation. If it has a student membership category, it's worth joining. Membership of the professional association in your country will not only provide valuable contacts and an indispensable source of information for your subsequent professional life, it will also give you access to professional translators whom you may need to contact for your research.

For a very useful list of translators' online resources – databases, discussion groups, websites, homepages and so on – see the *Translation Journal* 5(3), July 2001, at: http://www.accurapid.com/journal/ See also the list in Part IV of Hatim (2001).

2.4 Read Critically

Reading is simply processing information, and we can do this in a variety of ways. We may *skim* a newspaper to get an overview of the day's news. We may *gist-read* a report on university reform to understand the main proposals. We may *scan* a timetable in order to extract the detailed information we require as quickly as possible. We may *read* a recipe *repeatedly* if we're in the kitchen cooking a new dish. We may *sample* a history book to ascertain if it contains relevant information for our purposes. At the beginning of a research project we may *read* a key text in the field *intensively* in order to understand the various layers of meaning encoded in it. As a researcher you will probably use all of these reading techniques in the course of your studies.

Everyone reads for a purpose. Translators read texts in a different way from other members of the source/target language community. Lawyers read documents in a different way from their clients. It is therefore important to keep in mind your purpose when you read a text for the first time.

2.5 Take Full Notes, and Make Them Easy to Classify

You will need to make notes on everything you read. You no doubt already have your own personal method of note-taking. Some people use record cards, others prefer pads or notebooks or computer files. The most important thing is that your notes should be easily accessible. Have you tried using mind maps as a note-taking method? (See Buzan 1995.)

Generally speaking, you should make notes after you have read an article, essay or chapter. You should also make notes *in your own words*. This will ensure that you have thoroughly understood the text. Another reason to avoid close paraphrases in your notes is the risk of being accused of plagiarism. As a general rule you should note the main argument(s) – this will help keep your notes to a minimum and enable you to have an overview of what you have read.

In your notes, distinguish clearly between ideas that come from the source itself, and ideas that are your own reactions to the source, such as a reminder to yourself to compare source A to source B, who seems to disagree with A. Give plenty of space to your own written reactions as you think about what the source says. After all, the source is conversing with you, and your notes are your opportunity to respond. Are you convinced? Do you disagree? Has the source overlooked something you think is important?

As soon as possible you should begin to organize your notes according to themes; some researchers find it useful to code their notes, perhaps by colour or letters or numbers. This makes cross-referencing easier. Keeping full notes means including all the bibliographical information that you need to put in your list of references. (See 2.6 below.) Some scholars record all this information on a separate card or file, and keep their actual notes elsewhere, together with just a short indication of the source, in the form they would use in their final text (e.g. thus: Toury 1995).

It is also worthwhile to note the library code indicating the physical location of the source, in case you have to check something again later.

Be especially careful about recording bits you want to quote: quotations must be absolutely verbatim, and any omissions or changes marked, e.g. with square brackets. If you quote, check that you have understood the context of the original, and that you are not misrepresenting your source.

Here are some of the questions you might raise, in a critical spirit, as you read (based on Gile 1995):

- Are the author's objectives clear?
- Is the methodology explained clearly enough?
- Are the facts accurate, as far as you can tell? (Facts about dates and also bibliographical information)
- Is the argumentation logical, relevant?
- Are the conclusions justified by the evidence?
- Does the presentation seem careful, or careless?
- Does the author seem to be trustworthy?
- Is the author actually saying something important?

As you take notes, be aware of the differences between primary, secondary and tertiary sources, in terms of how reliable they are and what they can be used for. *Primary* sources are your primary material, your data or corpus: these are where you find your empirical evidence. *Secondary* sources are books and articles that other researchers have written about your topic, based on their own primary sources. You may want to refer to secondary sources to support your own arguments, or to borrow concepts or analytical methods that seem useful to you. But don't overlook important secondary sources that disagree with you: good research recognizes and explains such disagreements, and argues back at them. *Tertiary* sources are books and articles about secondary sources, such as encyclopedias and popularized works explaining and synthesizing other people's theories. They can offer you short-cuts and are helpful in showing you a general map of the land, but they are less reliable as supports for your own argument because they are so far removed from primary evidence. They are often a bit out of date, and may tend to simplify and overgeneralize.

However you record your notes, it will be helpful if you classify your notes according to themes or topics. This might mean using several separate pages or cards, each on a different topic, for your notes on a single source. In this way you will find it easier to group your notes for use when you come to the stage of converting them to a linear text: you simply collect in one pile all the pages or cards containing notes pertaining to your first section or topic, put them in the order you want to take them, then write them up; then proceed to the pile dealing with topic two, and so on.

See Fairbairn and Winch (1996) for an introduction to reading, note-taking and writing techniques.

Just remember: photocopying an essay from a journal or a chapter from a book and filing it neatly is not the same as reading it.

As you become more familiar with your subject and refine the focus of your research, you will be able to classify and evaluate the arguments being made: your reading will become more critical.

2.6 Keep Complete Bibliographic Records

As soon as you start reading and gathering information you **MUST** start keeping bibliographic records. This seems a chore at the beginning but with practice becomes routine. The main reason for keeping meticulous records from the outset is not primarily to satisfy some arcane academic regulations but **TO MAKE YOUR LIFE EASY.**

There is nothing more frustrating than reaching an advanced stage of your work and not being able to track down the source for an important argument or quotation.

It's best to cultivate good habits from the beginning and store your records in the format in which they will appear in the finished product.

At this point we need to clarify the difference between *References* and a *Bibliography*. *References* are works cited in a piece of academic writing; they are cited in two different places: once at the point in your text where you refer to a document (see 8.2) and then in a complete list at the end of your work. A *Bibliography* is a list of works relevant to a particular field and can form a book in itself, e.g. the *Bibliography of Translation Studies*. In the course of your research you will build a *bibliography*, but your work will contain *references*.

The references at the end of your text have two purposes:

- to provide the sources for the work of others which you cite and/ or refer to in your text
- to enable readers of your text to identify and locate works which you cite and/or refer to in your text.

There are many different ways to reference material and you

should ascertain whether a particular style is required by your University/Department. For standard international formats, including those for Internet sources, see the latest edition of the *Chicago Manual of Style*, or the *MLA Handbook* (MLA = Modern Language Association of America). In any case you should familiarize yourself with one of the internationally recognized styles early in your career as a researcher. The style outlined below is known as the *Harvard System* (or *Name and Date System*) and is frequently used in Translation Studies.

The *Harvard System* lists references in alphabetical order of authors' names at the end of the text. Where there is more than one work by the same author, these are listed chronologically. If there is more than one work in the same year, a letter is added: 2001a, 2001b.

The *Harvard System* has a number of different formats, depending on the type of reference:

1. Reference to a book

Here the sequence is:
- – Author's surname, initials.
- – (Year of publication).
- – Title in italics.
- – Edition (if not the first).
- – Place of publication:
- – Publisher.

Munday, J. (2001). *Introducing Translation Studies. Theories and Applications*. London/ New York: Routledge.

If there are two or three authors, all names should be given. If there are more than 3 authors, only the first name is given followed by *et al*. In the case of an editor, *ed./eds.* is added after the name:

Hatim, B. and Mason, I. (1990). *Discourse and the Translator*. London/New York: Longman.

Bowker, L et al. eds. (1998) *Unity in Diversity? Current Trends in Translation Studies*. Manchester: St. Jerome.

2. Reference to a contribution in a book
Here the sequence is:
- Surname of contributing author, initials.
- (Year of publication).
- Title of contribution followed by *In*: (italicized)
- Author or editor of publication, (initials, surname) followed by ed. or eds. if relevant.
- Title of book in italics.
- Edition (if not the first) or volume number if appropriate.
- Place of publication:
- Publisher,
- Page numbers of contribution.

Kuhiwczak, P. (1999). Translation and Language Games in the Balkans. *In*: G. Anderman and M. Rogers, eds. *Word, Text, Translation. Liber Amicorum for Peter Newmark*. Clevedon: Multilingual Matters, pp. 217-224.

3. Reference to an article in a journal
Here the sequence is:
- Author's surname, initials.
- (Year of publication).
- Title of article.
- Title of journal (italicized),
- Volume number
- Part number (in brackets),
- Page numbers of contribution.

Steiner, E. (1998). A Register-Based Translation Evaluation: An Advertisement as a Case in Point. *Target*, 10 (2), 291-318.

4. Reference to a conference paper
Here the sequence is:
- Surname of contributing author, initials.
- (Year of publication).
- Title of contribution followed by *In*: (italicized)
- Editor of conference proceedings (initials,

- surname) followed by ed. or eds.
- Title of conference proceedings (italicized) including date and place of conference.
- Place of publication:
- Publisher,
- Page numbers of contribution.

Mossop, B. (1994). Goals and methods for a course in translation theory. *In*: M. Snell-Hornby, F. Pöchhacker and K. Kaindl, eds. *Translation Studies. An Interdiscipline. Selected Papers from the Translation Studies Congress, Vienna, 9-12 September 1992*. Amsterdam: John Benjamins, pp. 401-410.

5. Reference to electronic sources

In the case of E-journals, the sequence is:

- Author's surname, initials
- (Year).
- Title of essay,
- Journal Title (in italics),
- Volume (issue),
- Location within host.
- Available from: URL
- [Accessed date].

Lindfors, A-M. (2001). Respect or Ridicule: Translation Strategies and the Images of A Foreign Culture. *Helsinki English Studies* [online], I. Available from: http://www.eng.helsinki.fi/hes/Translation [Accessed 12 July 2001]

In the case of mailing lists, discussion groups etc., the sequence is:

- Author,
- (Day Month Year).
- Subject of message.
- Discussion List (in italics)
- [online].
- Available from: Email address/URL
- [Accessed date].

```
Marc, P. (19 July 2001). Can MT rival HT? FLEFO
[online]. Available from: http://forums.compuserve.
com [Accessed 30 July 2001]
```

In the case of a personal electronic communication, the sequence is:
- Author's or editor's surname,
- Author's or editor's initials.
- (Sender's E-mail address),
- Day Month Year.
- RE: Subject of message.
- E-mail to recipient
- (Recipient's E-mail address).

```
Bowker, L. (lbowker@uottawa.ca), 5 October 2001. RE:
Corpus-based Translation Studies. E-mail to J.
Williams (jenny.williams@dcu.ie).
```

You may like to compare this model of referencing with the references at the end of **The Map**, which represent a variation on the *Name and Date System*. Conventions do differ between publishers as well as between university departments and/or degree programmes, so it is *important* to establish at the outset which referencing format you are required to follow. Whatever system you choose, the most important thing is to be consistent.

2.7 Plan your Time

The time available for your project is one of the most important considerations in its design.

If you are writing *an essay in the final year of your BA studies* you may have 4 - 8 weeks to complete the project. During this time you may well have other assignments to submit, so you may not have much time to do the research and write up the project. In such a case there is no point in deciding on a project which requires books/ materials on Inter-Library loan or the assistance of researchers/professional translators in other cities/countries.

If you are writing *a BA dissertation* you need to work out at the outset the actual amount of time you can devote to the project. By getting organized early, you will be able to obtain any materials and access to researchers/professional translators which you require.

If you are undertaking *a dissertation on a taught Masters programme* you may well have 3 months over the summer to complete the project. Not only is this very short, it comes at a time of the year when libraries may be closed and supervisors may be absent from the University on research leave or on holiday. It is *essential* to identify a supervisor and finalize your project design before the end of the teaching/examination period. Here, again, it is important to be realistic about what can be achieved in the time available.

If you are undertaking a project for *a research Masters or PhD* then time constraints may seem less of a problem. However, a 2-year or 4-year research project also needs to be carefully planned – otherwise there is the danger that it will not be completed.

Failure to meet a submission deadline may have *serious consequences*. You may have marks deducted for late submission, which could result in a lower grade; you may not graduate; you may have to register for an additional semester and incur fees. If you do not manage your time well, you may have to do a rushed job to meet a deadline and end up not submitting your best work.

2.8 Determine the Scope of your Project

Closely linked to the time factor is the question of scope. As we have indicated above, it is vital to ensure that your project can be done in the time available.

The *'Translation with Commentary'* (sometimes called the *'Annotated Translation'* – see 1.1 above) dissertation model is very popular on BA and taught Masters programmes in Translation Studies. One of the reasons for its popularity lies in the fact that it is a realistic option. It requires:

- a text that needs to be translated
- some background reading in Text Analysis, Contrastive Stylistics
- some background reading/ consulting experts in the area concerned
- an analysis of the text to be translated
- a translation of the text
- a commentary on the translation.

The text you choose to translate will in most cases not have been published before – if you intend to carry out a retranslation, then you must make a case for doing so. It is sometimes difficult to establish with absolute certainty whether a text has been previously translated. However, you should be able to demonstrate that you have taken all reasonable steps to locate any existing translation(s).

The *'Translation with Commentary'* model has the additional advantage that the finished product can be shown to prospective employers as evidence of your proficiency.

We would like to illustrate the question of scope with reference to two further examples:

2.8.1 The scope of a Translation Evaluation exercise

Translation evaluation is a valuable exercise at all levels in Translation Studies. Indeed, it is an area which is still under-researched and on which there is little agreement in the profession or the academy (see 1.2). At first glance it seems an attractive option since it limits the scope of the exercise to a maximum of two texts, the Source Text and the Target Text. As a result, students / researchers can easily underestimate what is involved.

Translation Evaluation requires

- – the presentation of an evaluation model, and
- – the application of that model to (certain aspects of) a text.

For example, it makes no sense to undertake an 'Evaluation of the Spanish Translation of Roddy Doyle's *The Commitments*' in a BA essay. Even as a PhD project this would be quite a tall order. In other words: in most cases it makes sense to evaluate *either* rather short texts *or* short sections of longer texts *or* specific aspects of longer texts.

2.8.2 The scope of a corpus-based Translation Studies project

Translation Studies has been quick to see the possibilities offered by the new technologies which have brought a new dimension to text processing and analysis.

However, building an electronically accessible archive of

texts which are sufficiently representative of a particular field may take several months of full-time commitment. You need time:

- to decide on the criteria for including texts in your corpus;
- to select your texts;
- to obtain permission from the copyright holder to use them for your research;
- to build your corpus – especially if you need to scan in material not available electronically;
- to pre-process your corpus if necessary (e.g. to align a parallel corpus or to annotate the corpus with part-of-speech tags).

Only then will you be able to exploit your corpus for research purposes.

If you are interested in working in the area of corpus-based Translation Studies but have only limited time to do your research, then use some of the corpora which are already available in electronic form (see 4.5).

2.9 Work with your Supervisor

In some instances you will have no choice about your supervisor. For example, the lecturer teaching your course may supervise all the research projects of the students on his/her course. Or the Head of Department will allocate you a supervisor depending on the workload of the staff in the Department. Or you may be attached to a Research Centre and have more than one supervisor.

However, in many instances you may have to find a supervisor yourself.

Ideally, a supervisor is someone who is an expert in the field you want to research, has many years' experience of supervising postgraduate students in Translation Studies, is reliable and conscientious, firm but fair and is someone whom you enjoy working with.

In the real world such people are rare and your choice of supervisor is also likely to be dictated by more mundane considerations such as your mobility, i.e. whether you are in a position to move to a different country to work with an expert. In actual fact an experienced supervisor does not need to be an expert in your exact field to be an excellent supervisor. And thanks to email and news groups, experts are no longer the inaccessible people they once were.

Every relationship between a supervisor and postgraduate researcher is different and evolves during the course of a project. Crucial to the success of the relationship is that both parties agree on how they are going to proceed with regard to:

- the role of the supervisor, i.e. hands-on or hands-off
- the frequency/length of consultations
- the time-scale of the project
- the methodology of the project
- submission of work and feedback
- the availability of the supervisor.

As the supervisor-research student relationship starts out in most cases as one not between equals, the supervisor has the responsibility to clarify these points in a sensitive and supportive way. Most problems in supervision arise because these issues are not discussed at the outset or not renegotiated at the appropriate time.

2.10 Emotional / Psychological Planning

Research is not a purely intellectual exercise; it engages both mind and body. And so research, like the path of true love, never runs smoothly. The steps involved in any research project – irrespective of its scope – which we outlined at the end of the Introduction, can be compared to the Grand National or any other major steeplechase event:

- the horse, fit and trained for the course, is on the starting line, all excited and ready to go
- it experiences euphoria as it hears the starter's gun and sets off down the course. It quickly settles into a satisfactory pace and then it sees:
- the first hurdle. This initially looks insurmountable and the horse wonders why it was entered

for the race in the first place and doubts whether
it will clear the fence. It does and is relieved to
find itself on the flat again. It runs along smoothly
until

- the next hurdle. This, too, is surmounted and the
  horse gradually realizes that this is in the nature
  of the race. The next few fences are negotiated
  reasonably well and then
- the water jump looms into sight. The horse finds
  itself in crisis, wants to ditch its rider and retire
  from the race. But somehow it manages the water jump and settles back into the race. Then
- the horse begins to tire – hasn't it done enough
  yet?
- impatience sets in – how much longer does it have
  to keep this up? Perhaps it could take a short cut?
  But there are no short cuts, so it ploughs on to
- the final hurdle. This seems much bigger than all
  the others. At last it's on
- the final straight, which seems, oh, so very long. It
  just has to keep going. Exhausted it crosses
- the finishing line, where rest and rewards await it.

The point of this rather colourful description is to alert you to
the emotional/ psychological ups and downs of undertaking research. While you cannot anticipate in planning your research
project what sort of hurdles you will face, it makes sense to think
of general strategies to deal with them. These strategies will vary
from person to person but will probably include identifying one
person or indeed establishing a network of people you can talk to
about your research, as well as identifying activities which enable
you to take a complete break from it. In alerting you to the difficulties you will face in the research process we do not wish to
underplay the enormous satisfaction and pleasure which research
will bring, both in terms of your own intellectual development
and the contribution you will be making to the discipline.

2.11 Information Technology Planning

By Information Technology Planning we mean that you need to ascertain at this stage

- what kind of hardware/software you require
- your own IT training needs.

TIP!

You may think that you need only word processing capability: but are you aware of everything MS Word, ClarisWorks, PageMaker or even LaTex can do? For example, one of the typical problems towards the end of any research project, especially a longer one, is the merging of different documents to produce the final product. Why not obviate that problem by creating a template for your project before you start writing? This could specify not only font size but also spacing, headings, sub-headings, pagination and so on. Can your word-processing package format your bibliography or generate a table of contents automatically? What about trying out citation software such as *Endnote5* (available from: www.endnote.com)? Maybe a refresher course on word processing would be a good idea?

Of course, certain types of Translation Studies research projects have specific needs:

- You may need to scan material onto your hard disk. Scanners themselves are fairly standard items of equipment but do you know which *OCR software* will read the characters you are working with? If it will read characters, will it also read tables and graphs?
- You may need *concordancing tools* for textual analysis. Which ones are the most appropriate for the kind of analysis you are undertaking?
- If you are working in the field of Multimedia Translation, will you need access to a *subtitling station*, a *VCR* or *DVD Player*? If you are analyzing dubbed or subtitled video material, can you ensure that you always have access to the same VCR? (Counters differ enormously and time can be wasted searching for a particular scene)

- If you are working in Software Localization you may need to run some *translation memory packages*. Is your PC powerful enough? Do you know how to work with such a package?;
- You may need *terminology management and extraction software* if your project is in Terminology. Do you know which product best suits your needs?

2.12 Keep a Research Diary

Some researchers, especially those pursuing higher degrees by research, find it useful to carry a diary around with them. Electronic ones are becoming more fashionable – although a small notebook/ shorthand jotter is equally as good. A research diary has a number of functions:

- A planning function: to set priorities for each week and note deadlines
- A recording function: to log your reading, writing and other research-related activities every day
- A reflective function: to note questions you need to reflect on as well as ideas which occur to you
- An organizing function: to list important contacts, opening times of libraries and so on.

Writing things down helps to bring order to your work and clarity to your thinking. Full-time researchers, especially at the beginning of a long project, sometimes find it difficult to cope with what seems like an endless, shapeless period of time stretching ahead of them. A diary can help structure your activities. By logging your progress, it can also provide reassurance at moments of self-doubt.

You can then review at regular intervals – say, once a month – what you have done, consider whether you need to rework your research question, set new priorities and goals for the next month. You will need to do this kind of "intellectual stocktaking" (Gillham 2000a: 24) on a regular basis anyway. Writing down your decisions helps to focus your mind.

Research diaries are very much a matter of personal preference. They are obviously more appropriate for longer term projects. We suggest you try keeping one for the first three months of your research project to ascertain whether or not it is helpful for you.

2.13 The Research Plan

Now that you have begun to refine your initial idea, established
your resource requirements and the time as well as the logistical
constraints you are working under, you can move on to develop
your research plan, which will probably go through several drafts.

A plan could be simply defined as "a way of getting from here
to there" (Yin 1994: 19). 'Here' is the research question, which
we shall discuss in more detail in Chapter 5. 'There' is the research goal, the answer to your question. Your plan will also have
to explain why you want to go there – this is your research rationale. And, finally, your plan will say how you are going to get there –
your research method. So, the structure of your plan might look
like this:

1. Introduction: your topic, its background and the significance of the topic to science and/or society
2. Aim and scope of the research: clear research
   question(s), and how you restrict the scope of your
   project
3. Theoretical background: brief literature survey,
   main relevant sources, main concepts and definitions
4. Material: what kind of data, where from...?
5. Method
6. Timetable / deadlines
7. Costings (if any).

The format of research plans varies enormously depending on
context and purpose. You may be required to submit a plan to a
potential supervisor, a Departmental Board or Research Commit-
tee or to an external agency such as a government department or an
international body. Plans vary in length and may or may not require
costings. Before drawing up a research plan you should

- Ensure that you fulfil the criteria for applicants
- Establish the exact specifications of the plan you are required to
  submit

- Draft your plan according to the criteria laid down
- Identify an experienced researcher who can give advice on your draft and help with any costings required
- Allow enough time to meet the deadline for submission of applications.

By following these simple steps you will ensure that you are not wasting your time or that of the person or organization you are applying to.

3.   Theoretical Models of Translation

Any research makes use of a theoretical model of the object being studied, either explicitly or implicitly. So if we are studying translation, or the translating process, we need some preliminary model of this kind in order to orient ourselves, to give ourselves an initial framework within which we can begin to think. What exactly is a model?

A model is a construction that *represents* some aspect of reality. Think of a miniature scale model of a car, representing a full-size car: it looks like a copy of it, but it is many times smaller. Or think of the way we can nowadays represent our planetary system by drawing a picture showing the sun in the middle, and the different planets at various distances from it. In earlier times, people would have drawn a different picture, with the Earth in the centre. These pictures are simple models. They represent their particular bit of reality by virtue of *analogy*: the round circle in the middle of our picture is analogous to the sun in the middle of our solar system, just as the shape of the model car is analogous to the shape of the full-size version. Note that this use of the term 'model' does *not* mean 'ideal'.

Not all models represent something in such a straightforward way as suggested by the examples above. *Theoretical models* represent their objects in more abstract ways; they are often based on assumptions about how something is structured, or how it might be related to other phenomena. These models are attempts to construct images of the object of study, images that hopefully make it easier to visualize, understand and analyze. Theoretical models are representations that are highly idealized and simplified; they are nevertheless useful conceptual tools. A theoretical model is like a map showing what are thought to be the most important features of the object. Different maps of the same terrain might highlight different features, just as you can have maps showing national borders or different vegetation areas, or economic maps showing different areas of wealth and poverty.

In your own research project, you might take a ready model of translation and simply use its framework and concepts unchanged, or you might adapt a given model to your own purposes. One of the things you might need to do, as you survey what others have written on your topic, is to compare the different versions of the models they used, critically evaluate their conceptual systems, and perhaps gradually develop your own version. You might even propose a brand new model.

So what kinds of models of translation do we have? Translation Studies has traditionally used three basic types of models: comparative, process and causal models. Each of these has several associated theories and variants. (For further discussion of these models, see Chesterman 2000b.)

3.1 Comparative Models

The earliest theoretical model of translation was a simple *comparative* one. It was static and product-oriented, centred on some kind of relation of equivalence. At its simplest, the comparative model looks like this:

Source text (ST) = Target text (TT)

or, if you prefer to start with the translation itself:

TT = ST

The equals sign, signifying 'is equivalent to', is a bit misleading, since we cannot talk about perfect identity in translation, of course. So the relation has been interpreted in many ways, in terms of some kind of relevant similarity. We can denote this by the sign meaning 'approximately equal':

$$ST \approx TT \text{or} \quad TT \approx ST$$

This model simply lines up the translation side by side with the source text.

This way of looking at translation underlies the contrastive approaches taken by scholars such as Catford (1965, especially pages 29-31) and Vinay and Darbelnet (1958/1995). The model sees translation as an alignment problem: the task is to select the element of the target language which will align most closely (under contextual constraints) with a given element of the source language. This is an approach that obviously has close links with contrastive linguistics, but there the model puts language systems rather than texts (instances of language use) on either side of the relation:

Language A/   Language B/
Source language (SL)   ≈   Target language (TL)

We can make a useful distinction here between correspondence and equivalence. *Correspondence* is a relation of (approximate) formal and/or functional equality between elements of two language systems (grammars). We might say, for instance, that the English adverb ending *-ly* (e.g. in *slowly*) corresponds to the French adverb ending *-ment* (as in *lentement*): the two morphemes have similar functions in the grammars of the two languages, making adverbs out of many adjectives. *Equivalence*, on the other hand, is a relation between two instances of language use, for instance two actual utterances or texts, such as a source text and a target text. In French-speaking Canada, for instance, you might see a roadsign saying LENTEMENT, but in Canadian English the equivalent text is SLOW, not *slowly*.

The comparative model is useful for charting equivalences, for instance in terminology work. Sometimes the equivalences of individual items are clear and one-to-one, but often they are not. A more complex case might look like this:

SL item X   =   TL item A (under conditions efg...)
                             TL item B (under conditions hij...)
                             TL item C (under conditions klm...)

Here, there are three possible equivalents, each used under different conditions. If we can state the conditions explicitly enough, we can formulate an *equivalence rule* for a given language pair. Such a rule would state that, under given contextual conditions, the equivalent of SL item X is...

The comparative model is also useful for studying shifts (differences, resulting from translation strategies that involve changing something). In this kind of research, we have source texts on one side and their translations on the other, and we analyze the differences between them. For particular items, or particular segments of text, do we find identity (ST = TT) or similarity (ST ≈ TT)? If we find only similarity, there must also be some difference (ST ≈ TT). What kinds of differences do we find, in what contexts? Do they seem random or systematic? If they seem systematic between two particular languages, can we formulate an equivalence rule? If they seem to occur regardless of language pair, might this kind of difference be universal? (For the study of shifts, see e.g. PopoviŨ 1970; Leuven-Zwart 1989 and 1990.)

A more recent variant of the comparative model is used in corpus studies which compare translations with non-translated texts of the same kind in the target language. Here too we have the same basic picture, centred on a relation between two entities, two sets of texts:

Translated texts ≈ Non-translated texts

The research task here is to discover the nature of the similarity relation, with respect to given linguistic features. In what respects do translations tend to differ from non-translated texts? If there is a difference (for instance in the distribution or frequency of a given feature), is this difference indeed significant? Is the average sentence length of the translations shorter or longer than that of the original texts? Is the distribution of different sentence lengths about the same in the two groups of texts? (For a pioneering example of research of this kind, see Laviosa 1998.)

The goal of all research based on a comparative model is thus to discover *correlations* between the two sides of the relation.

3.2 Process Models

The second kind of model represents translation as a process, not a product. It introduces the dimension of time and is thus a dynamic model. Some variants are based on the familiar communication model:

Sender (S) → Message (M) → Receiver (R)

We can apply this to the translation situation as follows, where R1/S2 represents the translator, at the centre of a double act of communication:

$$S1 \rightarrow M1 \rightarrow R1/S2 \rightarrow M2 \rightarrow R2$$

The Sender can be split further into original Writer and Client, and the receivers into Client, Publisher, and various kinds of Readers.

Juan Sager (1993) uses a process model to represent the main phases of a translation task, starting with the client's instructions (the specification), like this:

Specification $\rightarrow$ Preparation $\rightarrow$ Translation $\rightarrow$ Evaluation

Psycholinguistic researchers into translation make implicit use of a model looking like this:

Input $\rightarrow$ Black box $\rightarrow$ Output

Here, the black box (into which we cannot see) represents the mind of the translator, which it is difficult to observe directly. True, we can observe aspects of the neural functioning of the translator's brain; but we can only make inferences about the mind, on the basis of what seems to go in and what comes out.

We show these model variants in a simple linear form here, but scholars usually acknowledge that in reality the process they describe is more complex, with feedback loops, etc. (See e.g. Nord 1991.)

Process models are useful if what you are interested in is the sequential relations between different phases of the translation process. They allow us to make statements about typical translation behaviour, such as the micro-level use of time (e.g. the TRANSLOG project, see 4.3), or the temporal distribution of different translation tasks (Mossop 2000), or decision-making in a sequence of choices that we can represent as a flow diagram (following Krings 1986).

Process models are also used when the research focus is on the translator's problem-solving procedures. When problems occur (how do we recognize and define a problem?), what do translators do? What kinds of strategies do they use, in what order? How do they test and evaluate their strategies? Shifts can also be studied from this point of view, in which they are understood as strategic solutions to problems. Classifications of shifts or strategies are thus often ambiguous between process and product readings. For instance, 'explicitation' may refer to the strategic process of making something in the source text more explicit in the translation, or it may refer to the resulting product, the segment of the translation that seems to be more explicit than the corresponding segment in the source text.

3.3 Causal Models

Neither of the model-types considered so far are explicitly causal. True, they may well be open to a causal interpretation. For instance, a comparative model could be said to be implicitly causal to the extent that a particular equivalence relation can be read as a cause-effect sequence:

If X (in the source text), then Y will follow (in the target text)

In other words, X 'causes' Y, or is at least one of the causes of Y. Similarly, process models are also open to a causal reading, as soon as you say, for instance, that an output is caused by an input, or that what a translator does during a given phase is determined by what was done in a preceding phase, or indeed by the purpose of the translation.

However, in the above two types of models causality is not overt, not central, and not explicit. Comparative models help us to describe the translation product and its relation with the source text and with non-translated texts, and process models help us to describe the production process, but neither model helps us to explain *why* the translation looks the way it does, or what effects it causes. The questions asked by the first two models are 'what?' and 'when?' or 'what next?', rather than 'why?' Causal models bring in many more of the contextual variables we shall look at in Chapter 6.

At its simplest, a causal model of translation can be represented like this, where we use the symbol '>>' to mean 'causes' or 'produces':

Causes >> Translation(s) >> Effects

This illustrates that translations themselves are both effects (of various causes) and causes (of various effects).

Causality itself is a complex phenomenon, and can be understood in many ways. There are many kinds of causes. Some causes are deterministic and can be quantified (gravity causes things to fall, at a given speed); others are more difficult to identify and quantify, and we often refer to these as influences rather than causes proper (e.g. social pressures, literary influences). (See further Chesterman 1998, 2000b; Pym 1998: 83f.) In an attempt to reflect this range of causality we can refer more loosely to *causal conditions*.

There are obviously many levels or dimensions of causation that are relevant to translation. Here we will distinguish between three levels. The proximate (most immediate) one is that of the *translator's cognition*: the translation is as it is because the translator has so decided. Toury (1995: 249) refers to this level as the translation act, which takes place inside the translator's head. Here, relevant factors are the translator's state of knowledge, his/her emotional state, attitude towards the task, and his/her self-image as a translator, maybe even the translator's personality and life experience as a whole.

The second level is that of the external conditions of the *translation task*; Toury calls this the translation event. Relevant here are the source text, the client's instructions, the translator's computer programs and dictionaries, the deadline, etc.: everything that affects the concrete translation process from the client's initial phone call to the final delivery of the translation and payment of the bill.

The third level is the *socio-cultural* one. Here, influential factors have to do with norms, translation traditions, history, ideology, general economic goals, the status of the languages involved. Factors here may affect the choice of particular texts to be translated, or the choice by the client of a particular translator, or the decision by the translator to translate in a particular way.

Factors on all three levels have an influence on the final form of the translation, the translation's linguistic profile. But a translation also has effects, it, too, is a cause, an influence.

First of all, a translation has an immediate effect on its readers: something (presumably) changes in their cognitive or emotional state.

It may also, as a secondary effect, influence readers' behaviour. A critic or teacher, for instance, may read a translation, react emotionally by not liking it, and then write a review of the translation or give some negative feedback to the translator. Or a reader, on seeing a translated advert for a brand of chocolate, might go and buy some of that chocolate. These reactions are behavioural effects that can be observed.

Finally, a translation can also have effects at the socio-cultural level: if a great many readers go and buy that brand of chocolate, a whole economic sector might change. Translations can affect the way the target language develops. They can influence the way whole societies evolve, how religions spread. They can affect the way people think about translations and translators, and what they say or write about them: this is studied as the *discourse of translation*. Translations and people's reactions to them thus affect the status of translators in a given society. Translations can have a huge influence on how one culture perceives another, and hence on intercultural relations in general.

Causes and effects at each of these levels obviously interact and affect each other in extremely complex ways. Translators' attitudes, for instance, are influenced by existing norms, but they also simultaneously affect these norms, either strengthening or weakening them, and so help to shape their future development.

These different levels or dimensions of causality have led to different variants of the basic causal model of translation. Each variant highlights particular features of the overall picture. Some focus on translation causes, others on translation effects; some focus on the cognitive level, others on the level of the communicative task or the socio-cultural level. Below are some examples of concepts and approaches based on an implicit or explicit causal model.

- Nida's dynamic equivalence (e.g. Nida 1964) includes the idea of achieving a similar effect.
- Skopos theory (*skopos* is Greek for 'purpose') foregrounds one kind of cause, i.e. the final cause (intention), and skopos itself could be defined in terms of the intended effect of a translation. (For skopos theory, see e.g. Vermeer 1996; Nord 1997.)

- The polysystem approach and scholars of the 'cultural turn' use causal concepts such as norms, in both source and target cultures, to explain translation causes and effects; they also build in other causal constraints such as patronage and ideology. (For a survey, see Hermans 1999.)
- Gutt's application of relevance theory to translation makes explicit appeal to cognitive effects; he argues that optimum relevance (in the technical sense of the term) is the explanatory factor that accounts for communicative choices in general (Gutt 2000).
- Toury's (1995) proposed laws of interference and standardization seek to take us beyond description into explanation.
- Some protocol studies look for the proximate (cognitive etc.) causes of a translator's decisions (see e.g. Tirkkonen-Condit and Jääskeläinen 2000).

The long prescriptive tradition of translation criticism and assessment can also be seen in terms of translation effects. Viewed within a causal model, a translation criticism is the reflection of an effect that a given translation has had, in the mind of the reviewer or teacher or client. Prescriptive statements about what translators should or should not do are actually implicit hypotheses of effect, i.e. predictive hypotheses: they predict good / bad effects of particular translatorial choices. Reception studies also look at translation effects (e.g. Leppihalme 2000).

A causal model allows us therefore to make statements and formulate hypotheses about causes and effects, in response to questions such as the following:

- Why is this translation like it is?
- Why do people react like this to that translation?
- Why did this translator write that?
- Why did translators at that time in that culture translate like that?
- How do translations affect cultures?
- What causal conditions give rise to translations that people like / do not like? (What people...?)
- Why do people think this is a translation?
- What will follow if I translate like this?

And of course it is always possible to continue asking 'why?', for we can never arrive at all the causes or effects of something as complex as translation.

To summarize this chapter: you choose your model type according to the kinds of questions you want to ask and the kind of data you have selected; then you choose the most appropriate variant within that type, and adapt it as required by your own objectives. These choices you then need to explain and justify in your written report.

4.   Kinds of Research

This chapter introduces some of the major distinctions that are made between different kinds of research.

4.1 Conceptual and Empirical Research

Many scholars in the philosophy of science make a distinction between *conceptual* (sometimes also called: theoretical) and *empirical* research (see e.g. Gile 1998:70). The distinction goes back to the traditional debate between hermeneutics and positivism: hermeneutics (the science of interpretation) has often been thought of as the basic research method of the humanistic disciplines (philosophy, literary theory, aesthetics...), whereas positivist methods based on empirical observation and experiment have characterized the hard sciences. At its simplest, the distinction is between a focus more on ideas and a focus more on data.

Conceptual research aims to define and clarify concepts, to interpret or reinterpret ideas, to relate concepts into larger systems, to introduce new concepts or metaphors or frameworks that allow a better understanding of the object of research.

Empirical research, on the other hand, seeks new data, new information derived from the observation of data and from experimental work; it seeks evidence which supports or disconfirms hypotheses, or generates new ones.

Both approaches are necessary, in Translation Studies as in other fields. The differences between the two have perhaps been exaggerated by scholars taking one side or another. (See von Wright 1971 for an influential attempt to bridge the gap between them.) You cannot observe anything without some kind of preliminary theory (concept) of what you are observing: even what you take to be a fact or a piece of data depends on your initial theoretical assumptions about what would constitute a relevant fact in the first place; and any hypothesis must be formulated in terms of concepts of some kind. On the other hand, concepts that have no link to empirical data are not much use to science (however interesting they might appear).

Conceptual research (*conceptual analysis*) often takes the form of an argument. You might argue, for instance, that a particular concept should be understood or defined in a particular way; that it should be classified in a given way; that it should be related to certain other concepts in certain ways; or that it should be replaced by some other concept. One of the key words in conceptual analysis is (in English) the word 'as'. This term is at the root of much hermeneutic research. To interpret something, i.e. to understand it (so the argument goes), is simply to see it 'as' something else, usually as something more familiar. What is your personal concept of translation, we wonder? What do you see translation 'as'? Is it, to you, like making a cake? Doing a jigsaw puzzle? Performing a piece of music?

Conceptual arguments need to show that they are in some way more convincing than alternative or preceding analyses of the concept in question. An example is Ballard's (1997) argument for a particular way of defining and understanding what is meant by a unit of translation. Or Dollerup's (2000) proposal about how we should best use the terms 'support translation' and 're-lay translation'.

One reason why conceptual analysis is important is that concepts drive action: what you think (e.g. your concept of translation) influences what you do (e.g. how you translate). But conceptual analysis is also an integral part of empirical research, too. It involves processes like the following:

- defining key terms (X is defined here as Y)
- comparing definitions / interpretations by different scholars
- explicating and interpreting the overall theoretical framework, perhaps the basic metaphor underlying the general approach taken (e.g. 'translation is seen here as a kind of creative performance'...: what is meant by this, exactly?)
- setting up classification systems (concept X understood as consisting of categories ABC)
- defining the categories used in the analysis;
- deciding what to do with borderline cases, i.e. how to interpret category boundaries (categories interpreted as being black-and-white, or as being fuzzy, or as being prototype categories, or as overlapping...)

- interpreting the results of an analysis
- considering the implications of an argument
- coming up with new ideas that might lead to new research methods and results.

It is important to realize, however, that your selection and interpretation of concepts, metaphors and theories is not only determined by their empirical, objective applicability. It is also influenced to some extent by your subjective feelings, your personal ideologies and motives. Just as observation is never theory-free, so, too, theoretical concepts are seldom entirely value-free, entirely objective. Choosing particular definitions or interpretations can often be a kind of taking sides, of aligning oneself in one camp rather than another. This is what the writer Salman Rushdie means when he writes (1991:13) that "description is itself a political act". He is talking about literature, but the point is a more general one. Some translation scholars, for instance, refuse to talk about translation 'laws', as they feel this limits the translator's freedom of choice and denies subjective responsibility. Others do not like the terms 'target text' or 'target language', because of the military associations of the word 'target' and the way it seems to imply a model of communication according to which people communicate by throwing things at each other, as at passive targets.

Definitions of 'translation' that do, or do not, include free adaptations will also be influenced by the scholars' attitudes about what 'should' be counted as a proper translation, and perhaps influenced by their own experience, by the translations they have read, by the text types they work with, etc.

4.2 Characteristics of Empirical Research

Let us now examine some key principles of *empirical* research. (This discussion, and much of what follows in this chapter, is based on Chesterman 2000a and Gile 1998.) A good starting-point is the following quotation by the philosopher Carl Hempel (1952:1, cited in Toury 1995:9):

> Empirical science has two major objectives: to describe particular phenomena in the world of our experience and to

establish general principles by means of which they can be explained and predicted. The explanatory and predictive principles of a scientific discipline are stated in its hypothetical generalizations and its theories; they characterize general patterns or regularities to which the individual phenomena conform and by virtue of which their occurrence can be systematically anticipated.

Now look more closely at the key items in Hempel's statement:

First: *particular* and *general*. Any science seeks to describe particular instances of phenomena, but not only this: the aim is also to generalize, to abstract away from the particular in order to understand the larger picture. Some scholars in Translation Studies are interested in looking at what makes particular translations unique; others look for generalizations, patterns and regularities, even 'universal' features that are perhaps shared by all translations.

Second: *describing* and *explaining*. Any science aims to describe, yes; but explaining is a more complex issue. There are many ways of explaining something. We can explain why, or explain how, or explain what something is for. In other words, we say that we can explain a phenomenon if we understand its causes or the factors that seem to influence it; or if we know how it works; or if we know what its function is. We can explain it in some way if we can relate it to some general familiar principle; and in another way if we can analyze it down to its most detailed parts. In still another sense, we can explain what the phenomenon in question means, what its significance is. All these forms of explanatory knowledge can increase our understanding of it in some way.

Third: *predicting*. In the natural sciences, if we know the causes of something we can often predict when it will occur: it will occur when all the necessary causal conditions are present. However, explanations do not always mean complete predictability. We can explain why volcanoes erupt, but we cannot predict exactly when the next eruption will be, at a given place. Predictions, when they are possible, can be deterministic (100% certain) or probabilistic (less than 100% certain). In the human sciences, including Translation Studies, predictions are of course probabilistic. Given certain conditions, for instance, I can perhaps predict that most translators (of a certain kind) will opt for a certain solution, or a certain kind of solution, to a given translation problem. Prediction also has weaker senses. If someone slips and falls on the ice, we can say that we are not surprised: we could well have anticipated that *someone* would fall; and we can explain why they fell. Our prediction here simply lessens our surprise when something happens.

Finally: Hempel highlights the concept of a *hypothesis*. A hypothesis is a tentative claim, an attempt at a generalization, an attempt to capture an observed pattern or regularity. Some scholars in the human sciences use the term 'laws' to describe very general hypotheses that have turned out to be well corroborated; others prefer not to, thinking that 'laws' sound too deterministic and are thus more appropriate to the natural sciences. We shall have more to say about hypotheses in the next chapter.

4.3 Subtypes of Empirical Research: Naturalistic vs Experimental

Naturalistic (or observational) studies are those that investigate a phenomenon or a process as it takes place in real life in its natural setting. The observer tries not to interfere with the process (as far as possible), but simply observes it and notes certain features of it. This might be in order to get a general picture of what is going on (imagine you are observing the working habits of a group of professional translators), or you might have a specific question you are investigating. (How and when do translators revise their work? Do people work differently when working into or out of their native language?) The observer might also gather material via questionnaires or interviews.

In translation and interpreting research, useful observational studies can be done on the working procedures of translators and interpreters (see e.g. the project on professional workplace procedures outlined in Mossop 2000).

The very fact of your being an observer may of course have some influence on the behaviour of the person you are watching, but you just have to try to keep this to a minimum. Observation can also be done by video or tape-recorder, or even by computer records of keyboard usage. For a recent example of this, see the work done within the TRANSLOG project, reported e.g. in Hansen (1999).

The TRANSLOG program records every keystroke, and allows these data to be combined with a think-aloud protocol. The research design here thus involves what is known as *triangulation*: it uses three different sources of evidence, which can all shed light on each other: the translations themselves, the keystroke data, and the protocols.

Some naturalistic studies are *exploratory* in nature. They seek to analyze a situation or a translation without any specific hypothesis or initial focus. One result of such research might be the proposal of new avenues for research, new hypotheses. Other studies are based on more *focused* observation: a questionnaire study might ask translators how they deal with awkward clients. And still others start with a specific hypothesis which the researcher then sets out to test.

An *experimental study*, on the other hand, deliberately interferes with the natural order of things in order to isolate a particular feature for study and, as far as possible, eliminate other features that are not relevant to the research. You set up controlled conditions under which you test something. You can then compare these results with those produced under some other conditions, or those that occurred in a natural situation. For instance, you might want to compare the ways in which trainee translators revise their own texts with the ways professionals do. You therefore arrange two groups that do not differ (you hope) in any other significant way except trainee-vs.-professional, give them the same translation task, and the same deadline, and see what happens.

Many experimental studies have been done in interpreting research, examining how interpreters use different parts of their brains at different stages of the process, or how well they can understand or remember the source text under certain constraints, or how well they can work under conditions of extra stress, or how accurate they are. See for example the papers in the special issue of *Target* 7(1) (1995). Gile (1995) describes a simple experiment on the assessment of fidelity in consecutive interpreting, using a method that could well be applied in translation research.

In studies of the translation process, scholars have used think-aloud protocols under experimental conditions in order to find out about how translators revise their texts as they work, how they use reference works, how they are affected by their attitudes and moods, how they make decisions and solve particular translation problems.

For a recent selection of this research, see Tirkkonen-Condit and Jääskeläinen (2000).

In order to improve their validity, experimental studies often seek to minimize the necessary artificiality of an experimental situation. For instance, some think-aloud studies ask their translators to work in pairs, so that talking aloud will be more natural.

4.4 Qualitative vs. Quantitative Research

Roughly speaking, the goal of *qualitative* research is to describe the quality of something in some enlightening way. More strictly, qualitative research can lead to conclusions about what is possible, what can happen, or what can happen at least sometimes; it does not allow conclusions about what is probable, general, or universal.

For instance: Douglas Hofstadter's extraordinary book *Le ton beau de Marot* (1997) is built around a whole series of translations of a single French poem – around 70 in all, mostly into English, including some by computer programs. One of his aims is to show how rich the concept of translation is, as the poem can be translated in so many ways. He compares features of the translations; some he likes better than others; some have preserved more of the formal features of the original, some are both formally and semantically freer. Taken all together, the analyses provide a rich picture of the poem, both its interpretive range and its complex formal patterns. Having read them, one has a much deeper understanding of the poem itself, and of the complexity and potential of poetic translation. Hofstadter does not aim to state what is typical, or universal (although he does make some general claims about the translation of poetry); his primary aim in these analyses is merely to enrich our understanding of what is possible. He implies: look, it is even possible to interpret this poem in this way, and in this, and this... What does this new interpretation reveal about the potential of the original poem?

Quantitative research, on the other hand, has other goals. Here, the aim is to be able to say something about the generality of a given phenomenon or feature, about how typical or widespread it is, how much of it there is; about regularities, tendencies, frequencies, distributions. Ultimately, quantitative research may aim at making claims about universality. Quantitative research seeks to measure things, to count, and to compare statistically. Corpus-based studies are an obvious example (see 4.5 below).

It is often said that qualitative research is more subjective, and quantitative research more objective. This is true to some extent. Qualitative research often requires empathy (e.g. in interviews) and imagination (e.g. in discourse analysis). However, this difference does not imply anything about the comparative value of the two approaches. Many research projects have elements of both. The qualitative stage then usually comes first, as you set up and define the concepts and categories you need; and the quantitative aspect comes in later, during the analysis stage – for instance if you want to make claims about generality or compare tendencies. We shall return to aspects of quantitative research later, in Chapter 7, when we talk about representativeness and about using statistics.

4.5 Examples of Empirical Research Methods

There are various research methods used in empirical research. Here are some that are relevant to translation research.

Case studies focus on limited situations in a natural (not experimental) context. At its simplest, research material might consist of a single unit to be analyzed: a single translation, a single translator, a single translation company, the instances of translation in a single issue of a single newspaper. More complex case studies focus on several units, e.g. using a comparative format, comparing and contrasting different cases, looking for differences and similarities. (On the methodology of case studies, see Yin 1994; Gillham 2000a; Susam-Sarajeva 2001.) Because case studies are naturalistic, they involve many more variables than experiments (see Chapter 6 on variables). This makes them potentially very complex: you can never account for *all* the relevant variables of a real-life situation.

Case studies can be exploratory (what can we find out about X?), descriptive (what is the nature of X?) or explanatory (why X, how X?). A case might be selected for study because it is seen as obviously of special interest, a unique case (like the poem analyzed by Hofstadter, mentioned earlier); or because it seems relevant for a fruitful comparison; or because it is entirely new and therefore interesting; or because it seems to be a critical or typical case against which a theoretical claim can be tested. In this respect, case studies are like experiments: they are good ways of testing and generating hypotheses. A case study might seek to replicate some other case study, in order to see how strong the support for a given claim might be. A case study can also be used as a *pilot study*, e.g. to test a methodology.

A good example of a case study is Leppihalme (2000). Leppihalme starts with the mystery of why David Mamet's play *Oleanna* was so much less of a success in Finland than it was elsewhere. Her unit of analysis is the Finnish production of the play, comprising various subunits: the translation itself, the translator's goals, and the reactions of audiences and critics. She ends up with an explanatory hypothesis: that certain aspects of the translation were to blame.

Corpus studies use a wide range of textual data, containing many instances of whatever is being analyzed. For a very useful introduction to corpus-based Translation Studies, see Baker (1995) and the special issue of *Meta* 43(4) (1998). Thanks to new technologies, it is now possible to build very large archives (or corpora) of texts which can be investigated using concordancing software. In corpus-based Translation Studies corpora can either be *parallel* (i.e. containing translated texts and their originals) or *comparable* (i.e. containing translated texts and non-translated texts with a similar function and subject matter in the target language). To date most studies have investigated proposed 'universals' of translation such as explicitation and simplification. There is also considerable scope to investigate a range of relations between texts and their translations as well as between translated texts and texts written originally in the target language. Corpora can also be used as a resource for translators and a pedagogical tool (see the essays by Bowker and Zanettin in the special issue of *Meta* mentioned above). In addition, corpora can be used in terminological research, for instance in searching for a range of equivalents for a term or set of terms in a bank of texts or translations, before constructing a conceptual map showing how they are all related.

A major decision to be made here is whether to build your own corpus or use a corpus already available, such as the Translational English Corpus held at UMIST (http://www.umist.ac.uk/ctis) or the

GEPCOLT corpus at Dublin City University (see Kenny 2001). Do bear in mind that

(a) the validity of your results will be determined to a large extent by the criteria on which your corpus is built;
(b) building a corpus can be a time-consuming exercise;
(c) a corpus is a tool, i.e. the means of answering your research question, and not the answer itself.

For further examples of corpus studies, see several of the papers in Olohan (2000), and especially the one by Zanettin, who discusses many of the methodological issues of corpus design.

Finally, we can mention the survey study, and historical and archive studies. You would do a *survey study* if you wanted to explore or describe a phenomenon that is distributed over a population. Your research question might look like these: How many...? How widespread...? What kind of people...? Survey studies typically use questionnaires and/or interviews.

Historical and *archival* research methods are based on the exploration, analysis and interpretation of existing documentary and other information, such as bibliographies and historical records of many kinds.

4.6 Applied Research

The aim of *applied research* is specifically to make (or recommend) some good use of particular research results or conceptual analyses, for instance in meeting some social need. This is the kind of research that would be particularly useful for professional translators themselves, and for teachers. A good research design format would be the following (based on an idea by Emma Wagner, personal communication):

> Building on researcher A's claim that B (which was itself based on evidence C), this research will test the applicability of claim B to practical translation situation D. In the light of the results of this test, it will then formulate recommendations or guidelines for translation situation D, and if necessary revise or refute claim B.

The basic research idea here is to test a claim, a hypothesis. The claim being tested might be a prescriptive statement (such as: you should translate literally when you can), or it might be a descriptive one (such as: all translators tend to use a more standardized, neutral style than the source text had). The aim of this kind of applied research is thus not only to improve translation practice but also to improve the theory itself, by testing it against practice. It is thus prescriptive, but based on descriptive evidence. For further discussion of a project along these lines, see Mossop (2000).

Other applied research deals directly with issues such as translation policies in multilingual communities, language planning, translator training methods and issues concerning professional certification. In this research, the theoretical concepts are taken as given, valid and useful. They are then applied in constructing an argument for a particular recommended course of action or other application. An example is Agular-Amat and Santamaría (2000), who evaluate the appropriateness of different terminology policies in Catalonia and for minoritized languages in general. On translator training, see e.g. the papers in Schäffner and Adab (2000).

Other kinds of application include the development of electronic translation tools, dictionaries and helpful computer programs for analyzing corpora.

5. Questions, Claims, Hypotheses

The research process is like a dialogue with Mother Nature, or with 'reality'. We ask questions, and try to understand the answers we discover. As the dialogue progresses, we understand more and more (or at least, we think we do). One of the secrets of research is learning how to ask good questions. Questions then lead to possible answers, and then to claims and hypotheses.

5.1 Asking Questions

When you begin a piece of research, you have a slice of reality that you are interested in: in our case, we are interested in translation, in what translators do. So we begin to wonder about some aspect of it, to ask questions. At first, the questions are often a bit vague and general, but gradually they become more focused as the research topic is more clearly defined. One reason for reading the relevant literature is to discover good questions. Eventually, you should be able to formulate a specific research question or *research problem*. This final focus is usually something that gradually emerges from your work, as you proceed. Don't worry if it does not appear obvious at the start; just keep on asking questions and exploring, drawing mind maps for yourself, and then new maps... (On mind maps, see e.g. Buzan 1995.)

Initial questions are of several kinds. Some have to do with *meaning* or *definition*:

- What does X mean? How can X best be defined?

Answering this question might involve conceptual analysis, a kind of philosophical approach to clarifying a complex idea, such as 'equivalence'. This question could also be paraphrased: how can X be interpreted or best understood? This then prompts a follow-up question: interpreted by whom? This in turn might lead to a survey of what previous scholars had thought, or to a series of interviews, or even a questionnaire study.

Other questions are *basic data* questions:

- What can I find out about X?

This kind of introductory question leads to preliminary exploratory research. For instance:

- What was happening on the translation scene in eighteenth-century France?
- I wonder how professional translators actually work today?

Such questions then become more specific as the research plan matures:

- What literature was translated from German to French between 1740 and 1760, by whom, and for which clients?
- What use does a particular sample of professional medical translators make of Internet resources?

Then there are *descriptive* questions:

- What is this translation like, compared to its original?
- How can I describe what the translations by this translator/ of this text type seem to have in common?
- How are these translations different from non-translated texts in the target language?

Here again, the questions gradually get more specific as the plan proceeds:

- How has the translator dealt with place names?
- What are the relative frequencies of relative and main clauses in these translations and these comparable non-translated texts?

Still other questions have to do with *causes and effects*:

- Why is this translation like this, with so many errors?
- Why are there so many more relative clauses in these translations than I would have expected?
- Why was this novel translated and not that one?

- How did the general public react to this new translation of the Bible?
- Why did people react like that?

5.2 Making a Claim

As you proceed, you will gradually work out what kinds of concepts you will need in order to think about your basic research question. You will also begin to formulate possible answers to the question as you explore your data and read about what other scholars have discovered and proposed. These answers may be only preliminary ones, and will probably be refined as you go on. Eventually, you may be able to formulate good-looking answers as specific *claims*, supported by evidence and logical argument. Your claim is then your contribution to the field. If there is no claim, your work will just sound like a summary of other people's ideas or a list of facts or examples. You may arrive at potential answers and reasonable claims by logical analysis, or by painstaking examination of the data; or even by intuition, in a sudden flash of insight. Alternatively, you might start with a claim made by someone else, and proceed by testing it on your own data. (Is it really true, as Smith claims, that...? Contrary to what Jones claims, I will argue that...)

The next step will be to substantiate your claim, to test and evaluate it. (For more on presenting a claim, see Chapter 8.)

An example: suppose you are interested in retranslation, where a given text is translated again into the same target language. Here are some of the questions you might ask as your project proceeds, and the kinds of claims you might develop:

- How does this particular retranslation seem different from the first translation? (Your initial impression, which you will then methodically test.)
- What do I mean by a retranslation, as compared to a revision? (→ **Claim**: this is how to define the distinction...)
- Do other translations of the text exist, in the same target language? Who were the translators? Who commissioned the translations? Why? Where were they published? (→ **Claim**: these are relevant new facts.)

- Can I make any generalizations about the various differences I notice between the first translation and this retranslation? (→ **Claims**...)
- Does there seem to be a general tendency?
- How can I explain these differences / tendencies? Is there maybe some general principle underlying them? Is there a translator's preface or publisher's note that gives any clues? (→ **Claims** about explanations...)
- How do the differences I notice compare with differences noted by other scholars studying other retranslations?
- Some scholars have claimed that retranslations tend to be closer to the original than first translations: is this claim (known as the retranslation hypothesis) supported by my data?
- How do I test this claim? How can I define 'closer' in some way that I can reliably measure? (I can't measure everything, after all!) (→ **Claim**: this is a good way to measure closeness...)
- Is my way of measuring closeness comparable to the ways used by other scholars?
- Suppose I use different measures of closeness, or apply them to different sections of the text, and I get different results: how should I interpret these results?
- Do my results suggest that the retranslation hypothesis needs to be modified somehow, refined? Or even rejected? (→ **Claims** about the hypothesis...)
- Do my results suggest anything useful about methods of measuring closeness?
- Do my results relate to research in other areas of translation studies, e.g. on universal features of translation?

When you present your project and its results in writing, you need to state your basic research question early in the introduction, even though its final form may not have become clear to you until quite late in your actual research progress. You should also introduce your main claim(s) in advance, in summary form, so that the reader can see what is coming. Your report is not a chronological record of your work but a logical presentation of what you have achieved. In our example above, the basic research question could end up as something like this: Is the retranslation hypothesis supported by my material, if closeness is measured in such-and-such a way? On the retranslation hypothesis, see Gambier (1994) and the papers in *Palimpsestes* (4) (1990); for a refutation, see Susam-Sarajeva (forthcoming).

We have just referred to the retranslation *hypothesis*: a claim about a particular general characteristic of retranslations. In the philosophy of science, specific claims are often called hypotheses. This term is a standard one in the natural sciences, but is also used in the human sciences and in other disciplines. Let us now step away from translation studies for a moment, and take a closer look at the main general types of hypotheses (or claims or propositions, if you prefer). Each type of hypothesis relates to a particular kind of research question.

5.3 Four Kinds of Hypotheses

Much empirical research either starts or ends with a hypothesis (a claim) of some kind. You might start off with a hypothesis to test, or end up by proposing a new one. As mentioned above, hypotheses may arise simply from intuition, even in a dream. Usually, you slowly generate your own hypothesis during a process of thought and data analysis, after a period of trial and error. Or you can make use of a hypothesis that has already been proposed by someone else, and try it out on your material or test it via logical argument. To some extent, you are always making use of existing hypotheses, since it is not worth starting from complete zero for each new project. Why reinvent the wheel?

Hypotheses are important because they suggest ways of generalizing beyond the particular, ways of understanding better, ways of relating a particular research project to other work in the same area. Four basic kinds of hypothesis are commonly distinguished.

> 1. *Interpretive hypothesis:* that something can be usefully defined as, or seen as, or interpreted as, something else; i.e. that a given concept is useful for describing or understanding something.

Interpretive hypotheses are fundamental to any hermeneutic endeavour, to conceptual research; they are also fundamental to empirical research, as we have argued above. Consider a classic example: in

studies of Shakespeare's *Macbeth*, it is often argued that the three
witches represent the unconscious. In other words, the claim is that
we can make good sense of the witch scenes if we interpret them as
representing or 'meaning' Macbeth's unconscious. This is an interpretive hypothesis: a claim about how best to interpret something
or understand what something means. Attempts to understand something unknown often begin with an attempt to understand what this
thing is like, what we can see it *as* (recall the discussion of conceptual analysis in Chapter 4). Hence the usefulness of metaphors in
science – yes, even in empirical science. "Nonscientists tend to think
that science works by deduction, [...] but actually science works
mainly by metaphor" (Waldrop 1994:327).

Interpretive hypotheses are thus claims about research questions
having to do with meaning, definition or interpretation. Here is another example, from translation research. In a recent book, Michael
Cronin (2000) proposes what he calls a nomadic theory of translation. This is based on the idea that translators can be seen as nomads.
If we see them as nomads, as travellers, Cronin argues, we can understand many things about translators that may otherwise be less
clear. The metaphor provides new insights, allows us to make new
connections between different fields of experience (translation and
travel, for example). Cronin's research question therefore has to do
with how we can best interpret the cultural role of the translator –
what is it like? His claim is that it is useful and interesting to interpret translators as being like nomads.

As we have seen, interpretive hypotheses are the basis of all
conceptual analysis, all attempts to set up definitions and classifications of all kinds. Underlying them all is the claim that we shall
understand some concept or phenomenon better if we see it in a
certain way, for instance if we interpret it as being divided into
three types, or seventeen classes ... Translation Studies abounds with
interpretive hypotheses. Here are some of their typical forms:

- translation can be defined as... / should be seen as...
- there are two / five types of equivalence:... (i.e. equivalence can be seen as...)
- norms of translation fall into three classes...
- retranslation is interpreted here as meaning this:...; etc.

One weakness of our field, however, is the discrepancy between the huge amount of research that has gone into developing and refining conceptual tools by means of interpretive hypotheses, and the much smaller amount of research that has gone into applying these tools to real problems. We need interpretive hypotheses, but they are not enough for an empirical discipline. (See Gile 1998, and the distinction he discusses between theoretical and empirical research on conference interpreting.) Interpretive hypotheses nevertheless underlie all other hypotheses, insofar as they offer concepts in terms of which other hypotheses can be formulated.

> 2. *Descriptive hypothesis*: that all instances (of a given type / under given conditions) of phenomenon X have observable feature Y.

In technical terms, a descriptive hypothesis makes an empirical claim about the generality of a condition: it is an attempt to generalize. If you claim that all dogs have tails – that the condition of having tails is valid for all dogs – you are making a descriptive hypothesis, which we can of course test empirically. The claim that *all* dogs have tails is a universal, unrestricted claim; in other words, no conditions are set on the scope of the claim, on the range of its application (i.e. the range of phenomena for which the description is claimed to be true). Less general claims can also be made, about particular subsets of dogs, for instance. Here, the scope of the claim is restricted, and the claim is conditioned in some way. I could say that all the dogs *in my street* are friendly (empirical evidence: they wag their tails when we meet). Or I could say that all our *local* dogs are friendly *except two*. In both cases the descriptive claim is less than universal, but it is still a generalization: it says something about more than just one particular dog. The scope conditions define the range or subset of phenomena to which the claim applies.

Descriptive hypotheses are claims made in response to descriptive research questions. In Translation Studies, we find descriptive hypotheses (unrestricted ones) in research on translation universals. At a lower level of generality, we also find them (restricted ones) in research on particular translation types or text types, or language pairs. Because our field is a human one, descriptive hypotheses are usually formulated as tendencies rather than universal statements. Here are some unrestricted claims, with no limiting scope conditions (see the special issue of *Meta* 43(4) 1988):

- translations tend to be more explicit than their source texts
- translations tend to reduce repetition
- translations tend to be longer than their originals
- translations tend to have simpler style / syntax / lexis than non-translated texts
- translations tend to be more conservative / conventional than non-translated texts.

And here are some restricted ones:

- translations from German to Norwegian tend to simplify sentence structures (see Doherty 1996)
- translations of children's literature are freer than translations of many other kinds of texts (Huhtala 1995)
- professional translators use different kinds of reference materials as compared with amateurs (Jääskeläinen 1999)
- technical translators today, in Finland, tend to be paid more than literary translators.

Descriptive hypotheses aim to generalize, not to explain. The remaining two kinds of hypothesis both have to do with research questions beginning with 'why?', questions about causes and effects. Explanatory hypotheses start with the thing to be explained (the *explanandum*) and propose an explanation or a cause (the *explanans*):

3. *Explanatory hypothesis:* that a particular phenomenon X is (or tends to be) caused or influenced by conditions or factors ABC.

You might, for instance, wonder about a particular feature of a translation – say, its use of translator's footnotes. After studying the question, perhaps interviewing the translator, you might be able to propose an explanatory hypothesis for the existence of the footnotes. You might even want to generalize, and propose hypotheses that would explain the existence of translators' footnotes in general, i.e. the reasons why translators sometimes use them. Or you might start with the effect of a translation – say, its rejection by the client; an analysis might suggest possible reasons, explanatory hypotheses.

Predictive hypotheses, on the other hand, start with conditions that are thought to be causal, and predict the resulting phenomena:

> 4. *Predictive hypothesis*: that conditions or factors ABC will (tend to) cause or influence phenomenon X.

Predictive hypotheses can be used to test explanatory ones. If you have discovered, for instance, that certain features in a submitted translation have caused the client to reject it, you might want to predict that *if* such features occur in *any* translation, then the client will reject it. This is a prediction that you can go ahead and test. What you are trying to explain or predict might be some feature of a translation profile (e.g. an error, or a surprising abundance of relative clauses), or some feature of a translation effect (e.g. rejection by the client, quality assessment by a critic, reaction by the reader). Traditional prescriptive statements (such as: original metaphors should be preserved in literary translation) are in fact predictive hypotheses: they predict that if the translator does this, the critics and readers will like the result; if the translator does not do this, the critics and readers will not like it (recall 3.3) Like all predictive hypotheses, prescriptive statements, too, need to be tested.

The difference between descriptive and explanatory or predictive hypotheses is sometimes only a matter of how the hypothesis is formulated, within a given research project. If you are studying the retranslation hypothesis that we mentioned earlier, for instance, you could either take it as a universal descriptive hypothesis (all retranslations have this characteristic) or as a predictive one (if a previous translation exists, I predict that this new translation will have this feature, because I think the existence of a previous translation, plus perhaps the translator's familiarity with it, will have this kind of causative effect). In both cases, you could proceed to test the hypothesis on your data.

5.4 Hypothesis Testing

Good hypotheses (claims) must be both justified and tested, even though they might start life as an intuition or a dream. Justifying a hypothesis means explaining why you think it is a reasonable one in the first place, something plausible and interesting, worth testing. You might justify a hypothesis by argument; by relating it to other, more established hypotheses; by preliminary evidence; or by a limited case study whose results suggest that the hypothesis in question is indeed worth testing on more data.

The phase of hypothesis-testing is what distinguishes scientific work from other ways of searching for knowledge. Ideas, claims, arguments and hypotheses all need to be tested, so that they can be evaluated. Especially in empirical work, the first step is what is called operationalizing.

5.4.1 Operationalizing

In order to test a hypothesis, you first need to *operationalize* it. This means to reduce it to concrete terms in such a way that it really can be tested in practice. In their initial form, hypotheses are often rather abstract.

An example we mentioned earlier was the retranslation hypothesis, suggesting that later translations tend to be closer to their originals than first translations. The problem here is: what is meant by 'closer'? How do we interpret that in a way that makes it concrete enough to measure? In order to operationalize this hypothesis, we would need a very practical definition of 'closeness'. For instance, we might say that closeness could be measured in terms of the number of structural changes of particular kinds; then we would have to specify the kinds of change. Or that closeness could be measured by the number of semantic shifts or modulations per 100 words of the original; then we would have to define what we meant by these modulations. Another approach would be to use informants and simply ask their opinions; but you would first have to check that they all had the same idea of what closeness was.

Without operationalizing, you have nothing to actually measure; you would be limited to an intuitive impression. Such an initial impression might well have got you going on the project in the first place, but in hypothesis-testing you need to advance beyond this stage.

Another reason for operationalizing is to ensure the reliability of your research. That is, to ensure that your procedures are so explicit, transparent and objective that they could be replicated by another scholar, with a very good chance of arriving at the same results.

Decisions about how to operationalize abstract concepts, however, need to be justified carefully. Abstract concepts can be operationalized in many ways. We could measure closeness in many ways, too. How do we know that the way we have chosen is the best way? Probably we cannot know this for certain, but we need to be reasonably sure that the chosen method at least seems to be a valid one. Otherwise, we leave ourselves open to the criticism that our chosen measuring sticks are at fault, that they do not really measure what we think they are measuring, or that other measures would have been better, more valid. There usually remains a gap between the hypothesis and the concrete indicators that we use to test it, but we can try to keep this gap as narrow as possible.

5.4.2 *Testing*

Let us now consider the actual testing. First of all, there seem to be various degrees of 'testability'. The strongest requirement for an empirical hypothesis is that it should be *falsifiable*: it should be possible to prove the hypothesis wrong. For instance, a descriptive hypothesis that *all* ravens are black would be falsified by the occurrence of a single non-black raven. In the human sciences, most hypotheses are weaker: to falsify the claim that *most* people have two legs I cannot simply find a single one-legged person, but I have to make a statistical survey to see whether, in a representative sample (typical, non-biased, e.g. not made in a hospital amputation clinic), there are indeed more people with two legs than with some other number. Hypotheses formulated as tendencies are weaker still, for we can always argue about what we mean by a tendency. What percentage of instances (increasing at what rate over what period of time) would constitute a tendency? This is where we need inferential statistics.

If a hypothesis is not, strictly speaking, falsifiable, a weaker requirement is that it should nevertheless be *testable*. A claim that cannot be tested at all is not worth making, from an empirical point of view: it would be mere speculation. It may nevertheless be the case that if a hypothesis cannot be tested directly, it still has testable *consequences.* This is an important point when we test interpretive hypotheses. Because these are hypotheses about how best to inter-pret (understand) something, they cannot actually be falsified: they are not claims about the distribution or causation of features of empirical reality, but about the usefulness of particular ways of making sense of these features. Interpretive hypotheses are thus tested in use, by seeing what benefits they bring in conceptualizing the object of study. If they do not turn out to be beneficial, for ex-ample in facilitating fruitful analysis or generating new empirical hypotheses, they will simply fade out of use.

For instance, suppose you claim that it would be a good idea to teach translator trainees to think in such-and-such a way about translation: to think of translation in terms of, say, creative per-formance. This claim (an interpretive hypothesis about how best to understand translation) has testable consequences if we assume that *if* translators think in this new way, then their translations will be somehow different, perhaps better. That is, their translations will have different profile features – and we can then go ahead and test for the presence of these features, in comparison with translations produced by trainees who had *not* been expressly taught to think about translation in this way.

Hypotheses can be tested on four criteria: these are the ACID tests...

- ❏ **A** for Added value in general: new understanding
- ❏ **C** for Comparative value, in comparison with other hypotheses
- ❏ **I**   for Internal value: logic, clarity, elegance, economy
- ❏ **D** against Data, empirical evidence.

Testing means checking these things:

- ❏ **A**scertain that the hypothesis does indeed add to our un-derstanding of the phenomenon, it brings something new, it is not trivial, it is genuinely interesting
- ❏ **C**heck it against other competing hypotheses: in what re-spects is it better than others?
- ❏ **I**s it logical, elegant, parsimonious (economical), with no unnecessary concepts or assumptions? Is it plausible?

❑ **D**oes it accurately represent the empirical evidence? Does
it account for the facts? Does it cover a wider variety
of data, is it more general than competing hypotheses?

Whatever the hypothesis, it is worth bearing in mind that, strictly
speaking, a hypothesis can never be proved *true*, or confirmed to be
true. Science does not proceed by piling up truths, but by developing better and better hypotheses, which may well approximate closer
and closer to being accurate descriptions or explanations of reality.
An empirical test may support a hypothesis, or corroborate it; or it
may not support it; or it may falsify it. In Translation Studies the
results of a single test are seldom conclusive, one way or the other.

Hypothesis-testing often pertains to the *scope* of a claim. Unrestricted claims are maximally general, such as those proposing
translation universals. But most hypotheses specify a narrower scope
of application. For instance, someone might claim that the retranslation hypothesis only holds for fiction, not non-fiction. Tests might
then suggest that this scope is still too wide, and that the hypothesis
should only apply to certain kinds of fiction. Other tests might suggest the opposite conclusion: that the hypothesis actually has a wider
scope than fiction alone. Tests are thus carried out, among other
things, in order to determine the scope within which a given hypothesis seems to be valid.

If a hypothesis turns out to be supported by empirical evidence,
this of course might simply be due to chance, so a replication of the
test might be needed. Replications of hypothesis-testing procedures
are a standard part of empirical science, but so far they have been
relatively rare in Translation Studies. For a test to be replicated, the
methodology must be described explicitly, in enough detail. Different tests might also be warranted, to check the validity of the
hypothesis. A well-corroborated hypothesis can then lead to further generalizations, so that understanding grows.

If a hypothesis is not supported, this is usually an interesting
result in itself – and may be valuable – especially if the hypothesis
seemed to be well justified in the first place. Such a result raises
new questions. Was the empirical test perhaps inappropriate or not
sensitive enough? Was the material badly chosen, not typical, not
valid? Were the calculations wrong, not reliable? If you come to

suspect the test itself rather than the hypothesis, the next stage is to test again, or to replicate the test on other material. Or maybe the hypothesis itself needs to be refined, or even rejected?

A research project might start off with two opposing hypotheses, and see which gains more support. For example, one might test the claim that translations tend towards generalization and at the same time the opposing claim that translations tend towards specification (see Hermans 1999:62). Which hypothesis turns out to be better supported? Testing such claims would involve a comparative analysis of the underlying interpretive hypotheses, too: what exactly is meant by 'generalization', 'specification'?

6. Relations between Variables

Whatever bit of Mother Nature we would like to examine, we cannot possibly look at all the aspects and factors involved. We have to select some. What usually happens is that we select a few aspects and try to understand how they are related to one another. We are interested, say, in the emotional life of animals. We observe that dogs have tails, and that under certain circumstances (e.g. when offered food or patted) they tend to wag their tails. Cats appear to move their tails under rather different circumstances (e.g. when they are threatened). We arrive at this conclusion by studying the *relations* between the tail-moving and the surrounding conditions. Under some conditions these animals seem to do this, and under other conditions they tend to do that.

6.1 Relations

In many disciplines, the aspects of reality that we are trying to connect, as a way of understanding them better, are known as variables. We have just considered the relation between two variables: the occurrence of tail-moving, and environmental conditions that can be assumed to make an animal happy or angry. Furthermore, we have compared the relation between these two variables across two groups: dogs and cats. These aspects are called variables because they vary: they are not constantly present in the same way, nor do they necessarily occur in the same way among different groups. Dogs and cats do not move their tails all the time, nor are their living conditions constant. The tail-movements vary (in occurrence, frequency, degree), and the conditions vary.

A simple variable might only have two *values*, two possible states: we could say that a dog either wags its tail or does not wag its tail, there are only two possibilities. A sentence either is or is not grammatical, say. A text either is or is not a translation. Often, however, variables are more complex, more like a scale or continuum. Tail-wagging could be graded on a scale from 'minimal' to 'maximal', with many possible intervening states.

We could set out to study the variability of tail-wagging in two ways: either by setting up different conditions and observing how animals react to them; or by starting with observations of tail-wagging and checking the conditions under which this behaviour tends to occur. In this example, it seems reasonable to assume that there is a causal relationship between the two variables, in that presumably tail-wagging is a response to some aspect of the environment (rather than the other way round).

Causal relations are only one kind of relation. Another kind is a *correlation*: this means that two (or more) variables seem somehow to be interconnected, although not in a direct causal way. One phenomenon might regularly occur with or after another, without being caused by the first. (I regularly switch on my computer when I enter my office in the morning, but my entering the room is not a cause of my switching on the machine.) Correlations are not causes. The existence of poverty correlates with an abundance of donkeys in many parts of the world, but we cannot claim that the donkeys cause the poverty, nor vice versa. A third kind of relation is simply *chance*. In the tail-wagging example, we might initially imagine that there is no more than a chance relation between the wagging and some environmental condition; then we might notice that there seems to be a correlation, we see repeated patterns of phenomena that seem to co-occur; then finally we might suspect a causal relation: something in the environment actually causes the wagging. (In this case, of course, the situation is rather more complex: something in the environment presumably triggers a response in the animal's brain, which in turn causes a muscle to move, etc.)

Sometimes variability can be quantified fairly easily (number of wags per second...), but not always. Variables and the relations between them can also be studied from a qualitative point of view (recall 4.4).

Let's look now at how the concept of a variable helps us to understand something about translation research.

6.2 Text and Context Variables

As in any empirical discipline, empirical research in Translation Studies examines relations between variables. A variable, then, is simply something that changes within a given range of options. For instance, sentence length: we could decide that a sentence can be long, middle-sized, or short (and of course define what we mean by these terms). These three possibilities would then be the possible *values* of the variable 'sentence length'.

In Translation Studies, we deal with *two kinds of variables* – those that have to do with the translations themselves, and others that have to do with the world outside the translations – and we try to discover something about the relations between them. Roughly speaking, what we try to do is to see how aspects of translations are related to aspects of the wider world. A major problem is that there are so many variables to be considered. It is often difficult or impossible to exclude variables that one is *not* interested in, but which may nevertheless affect the results of an analysis.

Let's consider the two types of variables in more detail. On one hand, then, we have variables having to do with translations themselves, or texts that are assumed to be translations. These concern aspects of the existence and form of a translation (or set of translations), its linguistic profile. We will call these *text variables*. They can be any stylistic or syntactic feature, such as sentence length, use of slang, lexical density, text type, the distribution of particular structures, and so on. (For lexical density, see below 7.4.3.)

Variables of the second kind concern aspects of a translation's context. We will call these variables *context variables*. 'Context' is here understood in a wide sense, including anything in the spatial or temporal environment of the translation that could be relevant to it. Context variables can be grouped as follows:

- source-text variables (such as style, format, structural and semantic aspects, text type, the source language itself: all these form part of the linguistic context in which the translation itself is done, they affect the form of the translation)
- target-language variables (language-specific structural and rhetorical constraints; comparable non-translated texts in the target language)
- task variables (production factors such as the purpose and type of the translation, deadline, reference material available, computer programs used, relations with the client)
- translator variables (e.g. degree of professional experience, emotional attitude to the task, male or female, translating into or out of mother tongue)

- socio-cultural variables (norms, cultural values, ideologies, state of the languages concerned)
- reception variables (client's reactions, critics' reviews, reader responses, quality assessments)

So, what we do is look at the relation between a text variable and a context variable (or variables). Sometimes we might want to examine the effect of context on text: how are translations influenced by the various factors listed above? Or we might want to look at the effect of text on context: how do translations affect their readers, the target language, the target culture? We might also be interested in relations between text or context variables themselves: relations between lexical density and sentence length, or between ideological factors and translation out of the native language, for instance.

6.3 Variables Illustrated in Research Practice

Here are some examples of research projects that use different kinds of variables.

6.3.1 Martin Kaltenbacher (2000) is interested in comparing different machine translation programs working from German to English. Some seem to be more successful than others in translating particular structures. His text variable is simply the grammaticality of the translations produced, and his context variable is the computer programs: vary the program, and you get a different translation with a different degree of grammaticality. Like this:

> ST: *Er sah letzte Nacht einen Film.*
> Program A: *He/it saw last night a film.
> Program B: He saw a film last night.

The translations themselves of course also cause the researcher to react differently, to make judgements of grammaticality.

6.3.2 In English, some uses of *that* are optional. You can either say *He said that he would be late*, or *He said he would be late*. ***Maeve Olohan*** and ***Mona Baker*** (2000) compare the frequency of English clauses where *that* is retained with similar clauses where *that* is omitted, in translated and non-translated texts. The text variable is thus the presence or absence of *that*, and the context variable is the nature of the text in question, whether it is or is not a translation. Both variables therefore have precisely two values. The non-translated texts provide a norm against which the translations can be compared. Olohan and Baker found that the translations had relatively more occurrences of *that* than the non-translated texts. In other words, translators into English seem to over-use this item; they do not omit the optional *that* as often as they could according to the norm.

6.3.3 *Åse Johnsen* (2000) examines the Spanish and English translations of Jostein Gaarder's novel *Sophies verden* ('Sophie's World'). She is interested in how the translators have dealt with the references to European countries and well-known people and events in the Norwegian original. Her text variable is provided by the translations of the allusions, and her context variable consists of the source-text elements. Like this:

What Johnsen notices is that the solutions adopted by the two translators turn out to vary in a consistent way: one uses more footnotes than the other, one adapts more to the target culture norms (e.g. by changing the names of countries), and so on: each translator has chosen a different overall strategy. Johnsen then introduces

Context variable (= the ST)	Text variable (= evidence of different translation strategies)
Olaf den helliga	English: Saint Olaf Spanish: Olaf el Santo (+ footnote)
Norge, England eller Tyskland ('Norway, England or Germany')	Eng.: England, France or Germany Span.: Inglaterra, Alemania o Noruega ('England, Germany or Norway')

a second kind of context variable: the effect that these different strategies have on the way the translated novel appears in the two languages: in English it comes across more as a history of philosophy, while the Spanish translation presents it more like a work

of fiction. In sum: she first looks at the relation between the translations and their source text, and then at the relation between the
translations and their reception in the two target cultures.

6.3.4 Paul Bandia (2000) notes many unusual words and structures,
loanwords and foreignisms, in some French translations of post-
colonial African literature written originally in English. These are
the text variables. Bandia relates these first to source-text features,
showing how the source text also used very marked language, like
this (Bandia 2000: 359):

>ST: You cannot a thing I have done not put on my head.
>TT: Vous ne pouvez pas une chose que point n'ai
>accomplie me faire endosser.

The author in question (Gabriel Okara) allows his native language, Ijo, to influence the way he writes English, and the translator
has tried to maintain this textual strangeness. So we have a relation
of stylistic similarity between source text and target text. Bandia
then introduces a further point. He shows how both the original
writer and the translator shared an ideological motivation for
their foreignizing strategies. Both wished to foreignize their style
as a way of distancing the text from the language norms of the
former colonial powers, Britain and France. Bandia thus explores
the translation's relation not just with the source text but also
with socio-cultural ideological factors: two different kinds of
context variables.

6.3.5 Riitta Jääskeläinen (1999) used think-aloud protocols, where
translators are asked to think aloud as they translate. This can indicate something about their attitudes to what they are doing. One
thing Jääskeläinen discovered is that translators' attitudes seem to
correlate with translation quality: the more the translator feels personally involved in the task, the better the result often seems to be.
Maybe this relation could even be a causal one. In this research we
have a complex text variable and two context ones. The text variable
is a collection of linguistic features in the translations: a mixture of
stylistic and structural things such as overall readability, naturalness
of collocations, lexical choices, structural complexity (see p. 112

of her book). The first context variable is given by the protocol data, which includes evidence of the translators' attitudes. For instance, some of her translators made quite emotional comments sometimes, which Jääskeläinen interpreted as evidence of involvement ("... one of the most useless dictionaries..." (Jääskeläinen 1999:32); "... oh what a beautiful phrase..." (p. 233)). The second context variable is the reactions of the people asked to assess the overall quality of the translations as good, mediocre or weak. These people reacted to various aspects of the texts, aspects which they felt affected the quality of the translation, and made quality judgements. The researcher's task was to look for patterns in the relations between the three variables, and particularly between the two context variables.

***

In studying relations between variables, then, what we are looking for is patterns, regularities. We know there will be variation: that's what life is like, translations are always unique, up to a point. The exciting thing is to discover a pattern within this variation. People are pattern-seeking animals, after all (for an extended discussion of this, see Hofstadter 1997). Behind a pattern we might then find a principle, a law, which would explain it. A principle, even, that might connect this pattern to other patterns, perhaps according to some other, more abstract principle...

So when setting out on an empirical research project (and of course also when reporting such a project), you need to be as specific as possible about what variables you are studying, and what kind of relation you are looking for (or claim you have found).

7. Selecting and Analyzing Data

7.1 Kinds of Data

Translation research uses many kinds of empirical material. This material is mainly composed of *texts* of various kinds. In the first place, of course, there are *translations* themselves, and their *source texts*. Alongside translations there are comparable *non-translated* texts in the target language. Sets of texts to be studied might be defined by translator, by text type, by genre, by language; or you might want to take a single text and a single translation of it. Research methods will involve text analysis (also called textlinguistic analysis), and contrastive analysis if you are comparing two texts or kinds of texts.

A contrastive approach might also focus not on texts but on *grammatical structures* or *lexical items*, looking for equivalence rules for translating certain structures between a given pair of languages, or for terminology equivalents (e.g. for application in automatic translation programs). Here, the data are instances of the item in question plus possible translations of it: small segments of texts, in fact. Terminological research also uses data available in *term banks* and glossaries, as well as texts in special fields.

Research on translation problems or translation strategies also uses textual data: occurrences of particular problems in source texts, plus occurrences of the proposed solutions in the target texts. The data here are what Toury (1995:87) calls pairs of *replacing* and *replaced segments* in the target and source texts.

Other research questions select different textual features for analysis. Your data might be *textual indicators* of e.g. ideology and power relations. If you are interested in readability, your data will include textual indicators of readability and/or complexity. If you are doing an error analysis, the data are of course instances of errors, as defined and operationalized in some useful way. (On error analysis, see the special issue of *The Translator* 6(2) 2000, and the special issue of *Meta* 46(2) 2001.)

In some work, such as research on readability or errors, textual data can be supplemented with evidence from reader reactions: evidence of reading speed or text comprehension, or assessments of translation quality, for instance. This kind of data can be gathered via *questionnaires*, or *interviews*, or specially constructed *tests*. (An example is Puurtinen 1995.) There is a large methodological literature on both interviewing and the use of questionnaires. (See Gillham 2000b for questionnaire research in general.) Some research is based on interviews with translators themselves, recorded and transcribed. The data are analyzed as texts of a special kind: *interview recordings* or *transcriptions*. (See Cao 1996 and Sorvali 1998 for examples; see Gillham 2000c for research interviews in general.) Another example of a particular kind of textual data is provided by think-aloud *protocols*, sometimes supplemented by retrospective interviews and/ or by *computer records* of keystroke usage. (See e.g. Tirkkonen-Condit and Jääskeläinen 2000.)

Research on best practice originates in business studies; it involves comparing the different ways in which a given process – in our case, translating – is done in different companies or environments. The idea is to work out what the best way might be, by analyzing examples of successful and less successful processes. Successful examples can then serve as benchmarks in further developing the process. (See e.g. Sprung 2000.) The data here are operating procedures of various kinds, *actions* carried out by clients, translators and revisers.

Data used in historical research include texts about texts: *documentary material* concerning translations and translators, *translation reviews*, *translators' correspondence*, *paratexts* (prefaces, book covers, etc.), *bibliographies* of translated works, *biographies* of translators, and so on (see Pym 1998).

Finally, we can mention the data of a meta-analysis study. This is a systematic survey of everything that has already been done on a particular restricted topic. In a meta-analysis you do not take new data, but check through the results of all the published and unpublished work you can find, maybe reinterpreting it, evaluating the data and results of different studies. The aim is to arrive at an overall view of what is known about the topic, how well-supported a given hypothesis is, how comparable different studies might be. The data are thus texts again: *research reports*. A comprehensive meta-analysis might well be part of a PhD or a postdoctoral project. On a more modest scale, the literature review in any thesis is a kind of meta-analysis, in which you select and critically review the most relevant existing research from the perspective of your own research topic. You do this in order to justify the theoretical framework, concepts and methods that you have decided to use, and to establish the background to your particular problem or research question. This literature review sets the scene for your contribution, and highlights the gap that your work aims to fill.

Your data might be already available, but you might have to find your material or elicit it yourself. The finding or eliciting of basic data can take much longer than you anticipate. Translations can be ready, or they can be elicited. Source texts might have to be found. Or you might have to look for the translation of a given source text. Establishing a set of comparable non-translated texts is harder than it may sound: you need to ensure that the texts are indeed comparable with the translations you want to investigate or evaluate, in terms of subject matter, purpose and style. Setting up an extensive corpus is a major task in itself (see e.g. Zanettin 2000). Texts about translations and translators also need to be found, if they are not ready at hand. Newspaper reviews? Literary magazines? Bibliographies? Diaries? Historical works? Facts about translators might not be easy to find. Where could you look? Whom could you interview? Interviews need to be made, recorded and transcribed. This takes time – more than you might imagine. If you want to study workplace procedures, you need to find a few translators who agree to be observed. Questionnaires need to be planned, drawn up, pilot-tested, sent. Suppose few people reply? Ask them again? Then what? Think-aloud protocols need to be set up in experimental conditions, but first you need to find people who are willing to be your subjects, then you have to train them a bit in talking aloud in the way you want, so that they get used to it. Then the recordings have to be transcribed, which takes a great deal of time and effort.

7.2 Representativeness

Whatever your data, you need to decide to what extent it is *typical* or *special*. If your material looks like a special case, you obviously cannot draw more general conclusions about it. All you can say is that data of this kind are possible, they do exist; or you can claim that your data can indeed be interpreted in a particular way – because you have just done precisely that, you have interpreted them in that way. Special data might be extremely interesting just because they are so special. For instance, they might display some feature that was only latent or potential in other data, and thus open up new avenues of research that were not suspected earlier. Special data can also be useful for testing a very general claim: does the claim indeed cover this special case?

If you want to generalize from your results – i.e. to go beyond what your own data tell you – then you need to convince your readers that your data are not special cases but typical ones, representative of a wider population: perhaps potentially representative of all other instances of a given kind.

If what you want to do is test the validity of a general hypothesis, your data need to be randomly chosen from the point of view of the hypothesis. That means they must not be biased in advance either in favour of or against the hypothesis, so that the test will be fair. A good example of this approach is given by Maria Tymoczko's research (1999). She tests various general hypotheses (e.g. about foreignization) against data from Irish translation, and argues specifically that her data are good data to test the hypotheses on precisely because they are randomly selected in this sense. A general hypothesis applies to all instances within its scope of reference, and so any random instance within this scope will do to test it. The more test cases, the better, of course.

If the test results turn out to be negative, there are various possible interpretations (if the test has been carried out reliably). Either the hypothesis is false, or not as general as you had first assumed. Or the test is badly designed, not sensitive to the particular feature in question. Or the case in question is in fact a special case, outside the scope of reference of the hypothesis, and thus forms a kind of justifiable exception. To repeat our earlier example, you might find that the retranslation hypothesis does not seem to hold true for the translation of a play, or for the translation of a work of children's literature. You might then argue that these text types fall outside the scope of the hypothesis: this would in fact be a new hypothesis, with a new statement of the scope of the claim.

We can seldom be absolutely sure that data are indeed 100% representative. This means that most conclusions need to be qualified and made relative: you might propose some new hypothesis, or suggest that your analysis results are valid more widely, only *to the extent that* your data are representative.

7.3 Categorization

Categorization is a central element in all kinds of analysis, whatever your data. It involves two basic cognitive processes: looking for *differences* (variation) and looking for *similarities* (patterns). Differences may also form a pattern, so that there may be similarities among the differences. Looking for differences is a process of analysis. This means breaking a concept or a set of data down into smaller units; it needs concentration, convergent intelligence. Looking for similarities is a process of synthesis, of generalization. It means looking for regularities, shared features, patterns; it needs imagination, divergent intelligence.

Both these processes come together in categorization. The formation of relevant categories is indeed one of the most crucial and difficult parts of a research project. Categories are yet another form of interpretive hypothesis: you propose a category if you think it is useful, if it allows you to say something interesting, to make a valid generalization, to formulate a precise hypothesis about some part of the data. Classical (Aristotelian) categories are the black-and-white, watertight-box kind. You either pass an exam or fail it, for instance: here, there are two categories, and they are mutually exclusive and non-overlapping. These categories can be precisely defined in terms of essential features: if something has these essential features, it belongs to the category. For instance: if a student completes three of the four assignments and gets 60% or more in the final exam, the achievement might belong to the 'pass' category; less than three completed assignments, or 59% or less in the exam, would put the achievement into the 'fail' category.

In the past few decades, however, it has become increasingly clear that many of the categories we use in everyday life are not of this kind, but 'natural' or fuzzy ones, with fuzzy boundaries. For instance, take the category-pair 'young' and 'old': it is impossible to draw a precise dividing-line between them. Even apparently clear-cut categories like 'alive' vs. 'dead' are becoming more fuzzy;

nowadays we seem to have degrees of being alive or dead ('brain-dead', 'artificially alive' and so on). Natural categories often have a prototype structure, with clear, most typical examples in the centre of the category and less typical examples on the periphery. So we have typical birds like robins and blackbirds in the centre of our 'bird' category, and less typical ones like penguins and ostriches on the periphery (in the United Kingdom anyway: other cultures will have different prototypes). Fuzzy categories easily overlap with neighbouring ones. (For pioneering work on prototype categories see Rosch and Lloyd 1978.)

A related set of categories constitutes a *classification*. Here again, there are various options. A classification might be a simple binary one (colour film vs. black-and-white film, for instance). Or it might be a combination of two binary ones, as in a four-cell diagram, like this:

	Black-and-white	Colour
Dubbed	cell A	cell B
Subtitled	cell C	cell D

Another kind of classification is a continuum or cline, along a single dimension between two poles, such as free vs. literal translation. Such a continuum might be punctuated by various intermediate stages. Categories on a continuum tend to be fuzzy ones. A more complex classification might use more than one such continuum and thus be multidimensional.

The formulation of categories in a particular research project is determined partly by the nature of the material being studied and partly by the choice of theoretical model and its basic concepts. Because categories and classifications are interpretive hypotheses – other ways of categorizing and classifying a set of data are always possible – they too need to be justified and tested. Do they give interesting results? Added value? How do they relate to categories and classifications proposed by other scholars? Are they comparable? Are they explicit enough to be used in replicating studies? Do they represent the data adequately?

7.4 Using Statistics

Any research which adopts an empirical approach to Translation Studies – or includes an empirical study as part of a larger project – will involve collecting, processing and interpreting data. To do this you may need a basic understanding of some of the principles underlying the discipline of Statistics, although nowadays, of course, most of the calculations no longer need to be done manually. In this section we provide an introduction to a few of the key statistical concepts relevant to Translation Studies research. As an essential introductory textbook we recommend Woods *et al.* (1986), on which most of the following is based.

7.4.1 Random sampling
In 7.2 we drew your attention to the importance of *random selection* if you want to claim that your data is *representative*. In the field of Statistics *random sampling* is the recommended method to avoid bias in your data selection. The adjective 'random' sounds as if the process of selection is haphazard but in fact "a truly random sample can be achieved only by closely following well-defined procedures" (Woods *et al.* 1986: 72). For your sample to be truly random it must have the same chance of being selected as all other potential samples of that data. So, for instance, if you want to study a *random sample* of the translation output of a single translator who has translated 25 novels from English into Arabic, you might start by deciding that your sample will consist of 5 novels. This will give you a very large number of possible samples. In order to ensure that your choice is completely random – in the statistical sense – you will need to have recourse to a Table of Random Numbers, either in paper or electronic form.

You might, however, not be interested in representativeness at all. Perhaps the focus of your study lies in the translations of one particular author, or in the translator's early work or in what she says in prefaces, footnotes and/or afterwords about translation. The important thing is to be clear yourself about the principles underlying the selection of your data and make these principles clear to anyone reading your research.

7.4.2 Processing your data

Statisticians distinguish ways of establishing the most typical individual values in a set:

- The *mean* is the most frequently used measurement and is what is known in common parlance as the average, i.e. in order to determine the mean you simply add the values together and divide the total by the number in the set. So, if 10 translation students achieved a total number of 560 marks in a test, the average mark for the group would be 56.
- The *median* is obtained by arranging the numbers in order of size and then choosing the middle number. If there are two middle numbers, then the median is the average of these two numbers. Let us assume that the 10 students in the example above achieved the following scores: 12 40 40 42 48 60 75 78 80 85. The median is the average of 48 + 60, i.e. 54. The advantage of the median is that it gives a more typical value because it is not affected by extreme values at either end.
- The *mode* of a set of numbers is that number which occurs most often. The mode is useful in situations where the mean and/or the median give a misleading picture of the data – where, for example, your data are skewed in one direction or another. Let us take our 10 translation students again. Suppose their scores were: 38 40 41 42 43 43 43 85 90 95. The mode, i.e. the most typical value, is 43.

In most cases you will be using the *mean* to represent the most typical value in your data. The relationship between the mean and any other value in the set is measured by *variance*. One of the most important statistical measures is the *standard deviation*, i.e. the typical amount by which values in a set vary from each other. This shows how homogeneous a data sample is. *Standard deviation* can be used to calculate the relative value of any score in relation to the mean or in relation to any other score. It is therefore essential for the purposes of comparison – both within one set and between different sets of data.

Comparative studies are, inevitably, quite frequent in Translation Studies research. We compare (features of) source texts with (features of) target texts, different translations of the same source

text, the output of different MT systems. In all comparative studies, especially those involving human subjects, it is vital to ensure
that you are

- comparing like with like
- using an appropriate measuring tool
- applying that tool consistently.

7.4.3 Quantitative analysis

A number of quantitative techniques have been developed by researchers in the field of corpus linguistics to enable them to analyze
large volumes of electronically accessible text. Corpus analysis software such as WordSmith can be used to identify a range of textual
features which it would be laborious or impossible to identify manually (see Scott 2001):

- *Tokens*. The total number of tokens in your corpus is the total
  number of running words. So, if there are one million words in
  your corpus, then it has one million tokens.
- *Types*. The total number of types is the total number of different
  words in your corpus. In a given corpus, many words will be used
  more than once, so there will be fewer types than tokens.
- *Type/token ratio*. By comparing the number of tokens to the number
  of types, you get a type/token ratio which will help you to identify
  the degree of repetition in a corpus, i.e. the variety of the word
  forms. This ratio is also known as the measure of *lexical variety*,
  which is expressed as a percentage. The formula to calculate it is:

$$\text{Lexical variety} = \frac{\text{total types} \times 100}{\text{total tokens}}$$

- *Average word and sentence length*. Word length can be of interest
  in contrastive studies and sentence length can provide useful
  insights into translation strategies.
- *Frequency lists*. These show how many times each word appears
  in the corpus. While the most frequent words in a corpus are
  likely to be function words – conjunctions, prepositions, deter-
  miners and so on – a frequency list can provide statistical evidence
  (in terms of absolute and percentage occurrences) for stylistic

features such as key words in a text. WordSmith also has the ability to produce a 'keyness' score, i.e., to show how 'key' a word is in a particular text or corpus.

- *Lexical density*. This refers to the proportion of content words in a text or corpus and can be an indicator of genre or text type. The formula to calculate it as a percentage is this (see Stubbs 1986:33; 1996:172):

$$\text{Lexical density} = \frac{\text{total lexical words x 100}}{\text{total tokens}}$$

Before using the formula, you need to be able to distinguish the lexical words (nouns, verbs, adjectives, most adverbs) from grammatical/ functional ones (articles, prepositions, pronouns...).

- *Concordances*. A concordancer is a tool that lists every occurrence of a selected item in a text/corpus and usually displays it in context with a number of preceding and following words. It is especially useful for the study of collocation. Here is a sample for the keyword 'translation':

Canadian Association for Translation Studies, an association
orm for the promotion of Translation Studies as an academic
ernational newsletter of translation studies, is published b
lopments in the field of Translation Studies with special em
nificant contribution to Translation Studies, such as a doct

- *Collocations*. Collocations are sets of words that appear together more frequently than would be expected if left to chance. In the concordance above, you can see that 'studies' is a collocate of 'translation'.

See Kenny (2001:33-46) for a full discussion of these techniques, including their more problematical aspects.

7.4.4 Statistics – some do's and don'ts

1) Do have a clear understanding of what it is you are trying to measure.

2) Do make sure that you have chosen the most appropriate

means to measure it. We have recommended Woods *et al.* (1986) as an essential textbook. Depending on your circumstances and the type of study you have in mind, it might make sense to take a course on basic statistical techniques.

3)   Do present your findings in the most appropriate format: table, bar chart, histogram, frequency curve, graph. Don't forget to give absolute as well as percentage values – so that other researchers can have access to your data.

4)   Do think carefully about what your results mean. It is your responsibility as a researcher to *interpret* your results.

For further reading see Charniak (1993) and Oakes (1998).

8. Writing Your Research Report

Many books have been written on the research process in general, and on writing reports and theses in particular. This chapter draws heavily on Booth *et al.* (1995), *The Craft of Research*, which we warmly recommend.

8.1 Begin Writing Early, and Write a Lot, All the Time

You have a preliminary plan, and you are beginning to do some reading and thinking. You begin to take a few notes... The more you write, even if only for yourself, the easier it will be to produce your final research paper or thesis.

Think of writing as a form of thinking aloud on paper, as a conversation first with yourself and then with others. You write to remember, and also to understand. You write to distance yourself from your ideas, to get them outside your own head, so that you can examine them more objectively and clearly, so that you can see them in perspective, criticize and develop them. Sometimes you may feel that you understand something properly only when you have written it down; vague ideas become clearer on the page.

Writing summaries for yourself is better than taking photocopies – both for remembering and for understanding. However, do not make your literature review into nothing more than a summary of other people's ideas, as if you have simply been busy with the Cut and Paste options on your computer. You need to digest the ideas yourself and synthesize them into a coherent form. This needs genuine understanding and critical thinking. So show relevant connections between ideas, be critical. Try to make the various sources converse with each other, in a dialogue where you are also a participant.

8.2 Documentation Conventions in the Text

References
You need to document all your sources unless the idea is general public knowledge or something that you have thought of yourself.

In Translation Studies, the most common format for inserting references in the text is the name-plus-date system, together with the page number if necessary. These references are usually built into the text itself, rather than given in footnotes. You can either refer to the source as a person, or as a work. The bracketed information is usually placed either after the author's name (first choice), or after the reporting verb, or at the end of the sentence (if there are several references or a longer reference). See the following examples.

```
Toury (1995: 134) describes this as...
    [person]
In a later paper, however, Hermans argues
    (1999) that...[person]
In Laviosa (1998) the evidence discussed
    is ...   [work]
Several authors have made this point (see
    e.g. Gile 1995, Gillham 2000a, Yin 1994).
Snell-Hornby (1989: 45-69) suggests that...
    (cf. also Munday 2001).
Yet there remain a number of problems with
this approach. (See further Catford 1965,
Nida 1964, and especially Hatim 2001.)
```

In the above examples, note that references are normally given within your own sentence, before the full stop. If your references are given in a separate sentence, note the placing of capital letter, full stop and brackets, in the last example above. Placing a source in brackets gives it slightly less prominence.

The use of *see* suggests a direct source from which an idea comes or which makes the same point as you; *cf.*, on the other hand, suggests a less direct reference, to a source that can be consulted for comparison.

If you refer to A via a reference to A in B, and you cannot get hold of the original source A, you give this reference as follows, and include both sources in your list of references as separate entries.

```
Hempel (1952, as cited by [or: in] Toury
    1995: 9) claims that...
```

If you refer to two works by the same author of the same date, use *a* and *b*, as in Gillham 2000a, Gillham 2000b, both in the text and in the list of references.

If you refer several times to the same source, within the same paragraph or section of your text, you can use these abbreviations:

Kenny (op.cit.) [= Latin *opere citato* 'in the work
                              cited']
Kenny (loc.cit.) [= Latin *loco citato* 'in the place
                              cited', i.e. the same page]
Kenny (ibid.)   [= Latin *ibidem* 'in the same place']

If it is quite clear who you are referring to, you can omit the name and just put the Latin abbreviation in brackets, like this:

... blah blah blah blah (op.cit.)

Place references early rather than late, in the section of your text dealing with them. This makes it easier for the reader to relate an idea to its source, and not assume it is an absolute truth.

Your List of References (or Works Cited) is a list of all the works you have referred to: it contains all and only the references you have made in your text.

Quotations

Quote verbatim. Build the quotation into your own text, either separated off after a colon or introductory phrase, or as part of your own sentence.

Baker claims (1995:13) that "xyz".
Baker (1995:13) makes the following claim:
"xyz".
This is presumably what Baker is implying
when she argues (1995:13) that "xyz".

Indent, as block quotes, quotations of three or more lines. These quotations do not need quotation marks. For instance:

This is how Nida originally formulated this idea:

xxxxxxxxxxxxxxxxxxxxxxxxxxxxxxxxxxxxxxxxxxxxxxxxx
yyyyyyyyyyyyyyyyyyyyyyyyyyyyyyyyyyyyyyyyyyyy
zzzzzzzzzzzzzzz. (Nida 1964:170)

Quote only if the actual words are significant or controversial, if they are primary data, or if you want to appeal to the authority of the original writer. Otherwise, prefer paraphrases in your own words. Do not make your text simply a patchwork of quotations or a list of paraphrases.

Study the linguistic conventions for textual documentation in your own working language, in the research literature you read.

8.3 Think of the Reader: KISS and Tell

Writing is communicating: you write *to someone*. Your first reader is yourself, but the further you go, the wider the readership grows. You show a first draft of your work to a friend; then perhaps to other members of your group; then to the teacher or supervisor; you might present a later version at a seminar or conference; then you might publish a revised version in an international journal. At each step, the circle of your readers becomes bigger. The longer you work on a project, the more important this communicative aspect becomes.

As you start writing your first draft, therefore, consider the way your readers might react to it. What can you assume that they already know? From what point of view will they read your text? How can you arouse and keep their interest? Do you want them simply to accept some new information, or do you want them to change their beliefs or even the way they behave? You are not just writing, you are *telling* someone something – something you hope is important.

A research report is not a chronological record of what you have done, week by week: you are not giving a historical narrative in this sense. But you are telling a story of an intellectual journey, as seen and given shape by yourself in retrospect. The final destination of this journey might not actually have become clear to you until late in the day, but that's not how you report your work. From your chronological experience, with the wisdom of hindsight, you construct a logical story that will persuade your reader of the value of what you have done. Even though you may feel that you have been living in chaos for months, your writing task is to give a convincing form to this experience. The final logical shape of your work may only become clear to you gradually, as you proceed. Indeed, many forms of presentation may be possible, and you must try to choose the most effective one.

Readers like to know where they are going. So tell them their destination early: the main point of your work. They will expect the openings and closings of sections to carry statements or summaries of main points, because these parts may be the bits they will read first. Readers also like to know, at each stage, *why* you are telling them this or that – how does it relate to your main claim? Do you need to make this relation more explicit?

They like to be reminded of their route through your text, where they have just come from, and where they will be going next. So you need to use enough *metatext*, linking passages at the ends and beginnings of sections, signposts forwards and backwards. As you read what other scholars have written, take note of the kinds of set phrases of metatext they use, for the language you are writing in, such as:

```
As outlined above...
As we saw in section 1.3...
See below..
Before proceeding further...
At this point, let us summarize the main
steps of the argument so far...
Chapter 4 then deals with...
On the other hand, consider now a rather
different interpretation...
```

Readers like to be kept interested. If you tell them things they already know, or if you do no more than reinvent the wheel, they will get bored. If you are unclear, or leave out necessary information, they will get frustrated. On the other hand, they like a well-chosen, expressive phrase or a striking new term or metaphor that they might be able to use themselves later, with a reference to you: stylistic features like this give your text *quotability*.

Readers appreciate clarity, in argument, description, style and layout. It saves them time and effort. Clarity, however, may be interpreted in different ways in different cultures, and have different values: discuss with your colleagues and supervisor what it means in practice in your culture. At least in English it means you should

- Avoid a style that is syntactically complicated, with very long sentences
- Prefer active structures rather than passive ones
- Favour verbs rather than nouns
- Observe the *KISS* principle: *Keep It Short and Simple.*

Within a sentence or a paragraph, place information that you think your readers already know before information that you assume is new to them, or that is especially newsworthy: this is the *Old-Before-New* principle. (See e.g. the way the previous sentence was structured, with the name of this important principle coming at the end, as a climax.)

If readers start with a different point of view from yours, they will really need convincing that your point is indeed valid. They will expect you to be logical in argument, and they will expect you to provide adequate evidence for your claims. They also like to believe, unless there is evidence to the contrary, that what they are bothering to read is important to them, that it relates to a problem or issue they agree is significant. In other words, that it is scientifically interesting, as well as being personally interesting to you. Do you need to persuade your readers of this?

Your readers will not accept your claims if they feel they cannot trust you. If they think you are careless, that your tables do not match your text, that your calculations are wrong, that you have not shown enough evidence, that you have overlooked possible counter-evidence, that you have reported other research in a biased way, that you have missed important references, that you contradict yourself, that your categories or arguments are illogical, that you have plagiarized from someone else, that you are immodestly claiming more than is justified – then they will not trust you or what you say.

8.4 Show a Logical Structure

Research writing tends to follow certain structural conventions. This makes it easier for readers to see what is going on. A typical general structure might be:

>Statement of problem;
>Consideration of what others have said about it;

Proposed solution and evaluation of it.

Or:
Description of relevant background;
Statement of main thesis or claim;
Evidence in favour of main claim;
Consideration of competing claims and/or counter-evidence;
Conclusion.

Reports of empirical research tend to have the following elements, normally in this order but there is some variation:

Introduction of the problem, explanation of its significance;
Critical survey of previous research;
Presentation of the relevant theoretical framework and key concepts;
Presentation of the methodology;
Presentation of the empirical data (material);
Presentation and results of the analysis;
Discussion of the results;
Conclusion: proposals, implications.

8.5 Everyone Gets Stuck...

Writer's block is a common complaint. But there are ways of coping with it.

- If you can't think what to write next, spend some time going over what you have already written, giving it some stylistic polish.
- Draw a mind map of the bit you are struggling with, as a way of trying to see what its main issues are. Ask yourself questions about it. Where do they lead you?
- Look back over your research diary, for inspiration. Maybe you had a good idea last month, and noted it down? You do get good ideas sometimes, after all...
- Write a summary of where you have got to so far, just for yourself – just to get the juices flowing, to prime the pump. Stop as soon as you realize that you want to say something new.
- Write just anything at all, trying to explain to yourself where the problem is, and see where it leads you: this is a kind of thinking aloud.

Jeez, I feel really stuck today. Can't see how to get from chapter 2 to chapter 3 / how to decide about the methodology ... I read through a couple of articles that seemed relevant, but no luck. They were both arguing from a different starting-point, and their data were rather different from mine. They also seemed to have problems selecting an appropriate way of analyzing their stuff, but came to different solutions. Maybe I could discuss their solutions a bit, as a way of coming to something I can justify for my material... etc.

Just continue to type, and something will usually turn up. Talk to yourself in writing, but keep writing. At the end of the morning, you may have several pages of text that you won't want to use in your final version, but your ideas should be flowing better.

- Write regardless of style or grammar or typing mistakes – these can always be cleared up later. You may find that it slows you down if you focus on both content and form at the same time.
- Stop working on the section that gets you stuck, and start somewhere else that seems easier. No research reports, we guess, are actually written from beginning to end, in a straightforward linear fashion. People skip back and forth, writing different bits at different times, revising other bits, probably doing the introduction last, when they know where they are going to end up.
- Talk about your feeling stuck, with a friend, or your supervisor. Don't keep it bottled up inside you, but externalize it somehow – even in a picture. Then it's no longer part of *you*, and you can look at it from a different perspective. (Freud's advice, actually!)
- Go for a walk, listen to some music... take a break. Allow your unconscious time to work, to mull over the problem you are stuck with. If you have given your unconscious the necessary information about what the problem is, you can trust it to come up with some kind of answer. Sleep on the problem.
- Set yourself routines: a special chair, things arranged on your desk in a particular way...
- Get to know your own work rhythms. Some people write best in the mornings and spend the rest of the day reading as well as polishing their text. Others can't write until darkness falls. Knowing your own rhythms can help you avoid getting stuck.
- One way of dealing with the 'fear of the writer before the blank sheet of paper in the morning' syndrome is to always finish one

work session by writing the first sentence for the next session. This gives you a starting point for the next time.

- Set yourself achievable subgoals. A hundred pages before the summer sounds a lot, but suppose I think of the task in terms of pages per month or per week. Can I write 15 pages a week? That means two or three pages a day. That means a page or so before lunch, i.e. 10 lines or so every hour. OK, ten lines, then I promise myself coffee. Doesn't sound so bad, does it? – Write *something* every day.

- Set yourself deadlines! A factor that seems to correlate very closely with academic success and productivity is the ability to manage one's time. It is worth setting oneself deadlines and keeping to them: not just the final deadline, but intermediary ones as well. This should be part of your initial research plan. For instance, plan that you will finish the preliminary reading by date X, complete chapter 3 by date Y, finish the first draft of the whole thing by date Z. Intermediary deadlines could be set for each week, or month. When you do this, leave plenty of time for revision, and always assume that something will go wrong at the very last minute, such as a computer collapse or printer break-down. Keep back-up copies of what you write!!

- Look at yourself in the mirror and tell yourself, aloud, that you can do it. After all, you've achieved some other things in your life that you wanted to do, haven't you? (Don't laugh: try it – it works!)

8.6 Substantiate or Withdraw

Most academic research can be seen in terms of claims that are being made. A claim can take the form of a statement, an argument, a hypothesis of some kind, or indeed a statement or argument *about* a hypothesis (recall Chapter 5). One of the first things you will need to do when preparing your first draft is to formulate the main claim that you are wanting to make in your work. If there is no claim, your work will just sound like a summary of other people's ideas or a list of facts or examples. A claim, an argument, must be substantiated – supported by evidence and logic – or else you should withdraw it. If you imagine that, as you write, you are engaged in a conversation with your reader, you can also try to imagine the kinds of questions that will occur to the reader at different points in your text, to challenge your claim. How might you respond to these questions?

Here are some examples (cited from Booth *et al.* 1995:89).

Reader's questions	*Your answers*
What's your point?	I claim that...
What evidence do you have?	I offer as evidence...
Why do you think your evidence supports your claim?	I offer this general principle...
But how about these reservations?	I can answer them. First, ...
Are you entirely sure?	Only if... and as long as...
No reservation here at all?	I must concede that...
Then just how strong is your claim?	I limit it...

Apart from making a claim, then, you also need to provide grounds for it (evidence), and what is known as a *warrant*. A warrant is a general principle that explains why you think that your evidence is relevant to your claim. A warrant states or implies a relevant link (such as cause and effect) between the general kind of evidence you have, and the general kind of claim you are making. Warrants can usefully be paraphrased as follows (Booth *et al.* 1995:111-4):

> When(ever) we have evidence *like* X, we can make a claim *like* Y. (op. cit., 114)

You also need to qualify your claim, stating the scope of its application: how general is it?

Example (loc.cit.):

> *Claim*: It's been raining.
> *Evidence*: The streets are wet.
> *Warrant* (implicit): The streets are always wet when it's been raining: everyone knows that.
> *Qualification* (implicit): I mean it's been raining here, in this locality, within the last few hours.

Another example:

Claim: Translators tend to standardize their texts.
Evidence: 25 translators I studied translating three different text types shifted both very formal and very informal styles to a more neutral style.
Warrant: Using a more neutral style is evidence of standardization.
Qualification: My claim holds to the extent that my translators were typical, that the text types I studied were not unusual, and that style shifts of this kind can indeed be interpreted as evidence of standardization. There are thus limits to the extent that I can generalize from my results.

Desirable features of claims are that they should be specific, explicit enough to be tested, and important enough to deserve our attention. Important claims are those that somehow contradict or disturb the existing state of knowledge. For instance, an important claim might be:

- that some previous research has made a factual error;
- that you have discovered some important new facts;
- that you have discovered an error in reasoning in some previous research;
- that you have discovered some counter-evidence or counter-argument to a previous claim;
- that a particular hypothesis needs to be formulated differently;
- that you have discovered a much better way of describing something, or of analyzing something, or of explaining something.

With respect to qualifications, one important aspect of academic writing is the use of *hedges*. A hedge is a sign of academic modesty: it says 'I'm not absolutely sure that X, but it seems likely or possible, based on my evidence'. Typical hedges in English are:

perhaps, seem, appear, to some extent, insofar as, possibly, may, some example (i.e. not all), *in many cases* (i.e. not all).

Qualifications take into account possible objections that your readers might raise. You can protect yourself against these objections by anticipating them:

- by defining your key terms carefully, to avoid objections based on misunderstanding
- by showing that you are aware of the risk of oversimplifying causes and effects
- by being careful not to overgeneralize on the basis of too little or non-representative (non-typical) evidence
- by considering possible counter-examples, counter-evidence and special cases.

Other qualifications stipulate the limiting conditions under which you think your claim holds and thus restrict its scope (e.g. "this claim holds only for the translation of children's literature / only for the translation of advertisements in Eastern European countries in the period 1980-2000").

You may have to concede some objections in advance. Doing this at least shows that you are aware of them, aware of some weaknesses in your work; it also shows that you know further work will be necessary.

8.7 Starting and Finishing

You might draft your *introduction* quite early, but it will probably be the last thing you revise into its final form. It will be one of the first bits the reader looks at. Here, you need to catch the readers' interest, and persuade them that it is worth reading further.

Introductions in good academic writing tend to follow fairly standard patterns, consisting of particular rhetorical moves. (See Booth *et al.* 1995:234-254.)

> *Move 1: Call for attention.* Start with something that will catch the reader's attention: think carefully about your very first sentence. A neat quotation? A rhetorical question? A dramatic statement that will surprise readers? A curious fact? An anecdote? A general statement? A joke? Something that connects to the title of your work? (Do you have a memorable title? Perhaps also an informative secondary title?)

Move 2: Give the context. Then provide some kind of general context for your work: put the reader in the picture, make it clear what you are assuming is generally understood, what kind of field we are dealing with here. This stakes out the common ground that you want your reader to share with you. It might include a brief reference to some relevant previous research.

Move 3: State the problem. This move narrows the focus down to the particular theme of your work, the knowledge gap that needs to be filled, the problem that you want to solve, the misunderstanding or disagreement or contradiction that needs to be resolved.

Move 4. Justify your work. This move states the motivation for your work, why you think it is important: why does your research question need to be answered? Why is it worth studying?

Move 5: State your aim. Now comes the first statement of the main point of your work, what you are aiming to do. You might give a succinct statement of your main argument, or anticipate your main results.

Introductions often then end with a brief preview of how the article or thesis will be organized, so that readers have a rough map as they set out through the text.

There is plenty of room for flexibility in how the moves are realized; check them out against the introductions of some of the articles you are reading. How are these moves realized in introductions that you think are particularly effective or ineffective? Do the moves always come in this order? Are they all always present? Do they seem separate, or combined?

Conclusions are in a sense mirror images of introductions. In other words, they typically move out from the particular research problem to the wider context again. Typical moves are the following:

Move 1: Look back. Restate your main point again, your main results. (Check that your key terms here match with those you introduced in the introduction.) Remember that your conclusion section may be the first thing the reader looks at after seeing your title.

Move 2: Claim significance. Explain why you think your work, or some aspect of it, is valuable. Does it have implications for theoretical development? Does it have practical applications? Here, you try to answer the reader's question: 'so what?' Recall the way in which you formulated your research proposal during the planning stage, and justified your plan. Show what consequences your work might have.

Move 3: Assess your own work. Be self-critical and realistically modest about what you have achieved, claiming your own strengths and acknowledging weaknesses. Disarm potential critics by admitting possible defects, limited or perhaps not representative data, weak correlations, etc. This is an important move in theses.

Move 4: Suggest follow-up research. What should be done next, either by you or by some other researcher who is interested in this topic? Where is more research needed? What new problems arise as a result of your work?

Move 5: Add a coda. Some writers like to end with a rhetorical flourish that will stick in the reader's mind.

8.8 Feedback and Revision

Writing is not a linear process, but it is certainly a process. Be prepared to compose lots of successive drafts, and to revise them heavily. Einstein apparently once said that all you need in order to do great research is paper, a pencil and a wastepaper basket, and by far the most important of these is the wastepaper basket. In other words, be prepared to throw away a lot of what you write.

Fish for feedback as often as you can, from friends, peers, teachers and supervisors. Research is a communal activity, based on dialogue. If you submit an article for publication, the editors and referees will provide critical feedback. If it is eventually published, your peers may also respond to it. We never arrive at final truths, but we do hope we can get better understanding.

When you revise your text, especially during the final stages, it is worth checking it through from four different points of view.

Overall structure and logic: Try to read your text as a reader might who sees it now for the first time. Are you giving the reader enough relevant information at each point? Is your main point clear?

Reader-friendliness: Are you clear enough, explicit enough? Key definitions OK? Concepts and categories explained? Enough variation to make your style interesting? Too many complex sentences? Consistent terminology? Enough metatext? Are there enough transitions, is the reader adequately guided from one section to the next? Enough recapitulation of main points?

Proof-reading: Check separately for typing and grammar errors, missing words, incorrect numbers and dates, etc. Don't forget to use the spell-checker in your word-processing package BUT don't rely on it: it cannot distinguish between *their* and *there*, between *though*, *through* and *thorough*.

Visual aspect: Is the layout optimal? Are the sections correctly numbered, do they correspond to the list of contents? Are tables and graphs clear, not misleading, correctly labelled? Use of italics and boldface, different fonts? Presentation and numbering of examples?

Try to tell your story as well as possible, but also be realistic. According to Murphy's Law, when you see your work in print at last, the first thing you notice will be a misprint.

9.   Presenting Your Research Orally

As a researcher you may be required to present your work orally in a variety of different contexts. For example, you may:

- give a seminar paper to your classmates
- present your progress as a researcher after your first year of registration – perhaps as part of a transfer procedure from MA to PhD;
- give a paper at a Translation Studies conference
- make a presentation on your research to a potential employer
- present your research as part of the examining process, as in a viva
- deliver an invited lecture.

PREPARATION is the key to a good oral performance. Good presentations take time to prepare. Mark Twain is credited with the assertion that "it takes three weeks to prepare a good ad-lib speech". Ideas take time to evolve and creativity cannot be rushed – last-minute preparation rarely produces a good performance.

The first task is to *identify your audience* and their level of expertise: are they experts in the area of Translation Studies you plan to talk about? Are they experts in other areas of Translation Studies? What level of knowledge (if any) do they have? A potential employer may know next to nothing about Translation Studies whereas an External Examiner for a doctoral thesis can be expected to know a lot.

The *purpose of your talk* is the second important consideration at this point. While the primary purpose is in most cases to *inform* your audience about the results of your research, you may also need to *persuade* (your examiners to accept your doctoral thesis), to *entertain* (an audience at an invited lecture) or to *establish credibility* (with a potential employer).

Equipped with the knowledge of WHO you are addressing and WHY you are addressing them, you can now begin to plan WHAT you are going to say. We are assuming here that you have something worthwhile to say. If that is not the case, e.g. if your research has not yet produced results worth reporting, then it is better not to offer a conference paper or accept an invitation to give a lecture. By doing so you will not waste your own time and that of others.

The content of your presentation will be limited by the time at your disposal. A *Golden Rule* of making oral presentations is: *Never exceed the allotted time*. Doing so usually means that you have to omit or rush the most important part of your presentation: the conclusion. Furthermore, if you are one of a series of presenters your inability to finish on time will annoy not only other presenters but also the organisers of the event since their carefully planned schedule will slowly fall apart. Your audience, too, may lose interest if your presentation comes before a lunch or coffee break.

Oral presentations may last 20 minutes (e.g. a conference paper), 30 minutes (e.g. a presentation to classmates, a potential employer or a Research Progression Board) or 45 minutes (e.g. an invited lecture). In addition, there will usually be a period after your presentation set aside for questions and answers.

An oral presentation differs from an essay or other written piece of work in two important ways:

1. The audience has only *one chance* to hear what you have to say;
2. You are communicating *directly* with your audience.

Since your audience will hear you only once, *don't try to say too much* and *make it easy for your audience to follow you.*

Your presentation should have a maximum of between 3 and 5 main points, depending on the time at your disposal. You can make the content of your presentation easy for your audience to follow by *structuring it well*, *delivering it well* and *using visual aids well.*

9.1 Structure

A piece of advice frequently cited in the literature (e.g. Anholt 1994; Leigh and Maynard 1999) is: *Tell 'em what you're gonna tell 'em, then tell 'em, then tell 'em what you've told 'em'*. In other words, presentations should have 3 sections:

1. *A beginning* (which gives the background to the presentation and states the question being researched and/or the hypothesis being tested or proposed);

2. *A middle* (which gives the new data or the new ideas arising from your research);
3. *An end* (which summarizes the results of your research and provides a conclusion).

The conclusion is a very important – if not the most important – part of your presentation as it is what will remain with the audience after the event: it should therefore be concise and to the point.

Your presentation should be relevant, coherent and succinct. If, for instance, you are required to present in 30 minutes the results of your first year's work as a doctoral student in Translation History, your presentation might have the following structure:

1. Your initial research question(s) might have been about the factors influencing successive translations of a given text in English. Any relevant studies should be mentioned here;
2. How/why you decided to concentrate on text X and why you decided to prioritize one factor, e.g. the translator(s). The initial findings of this approach;
3. A conclusion about your methodology, initial results and future plans.

There is no need to include a discussion of all the other texts / factors you rejected along the way. In this situation the assessors want to know (a) that your project is well focused, (b) that your methodology is sound, and (c) that you are intellectually capable of completing the project.

9.2 Delivery

Keep in mind that in presenting your research orally you are entering into *dialogue* with your audience. The reception of what you say depends not only on WHAT you are saying but also on HOW you are presenting it.

Whether you give your talk based on a few notes or on a complete script or on something in-between varies according to the individual. Find out which method is most comfortable for you. If you prefer to have your presentation written out in full in advance, don't forget to 'translate' it into an oral style. Texts written to be read silently are very different from texts written to be read aloud. When delivering your presentation it is important to:

- Speak directly to your audience, maintaining eye contact. This shows that you are interested in them and helps you to gauge their reaction. *Never* read a script held in front of your nose – this is extremely difficult for an audience to follow.
- Use a range of rhetorical devices to avoid monotony: vary the tone and volume of your voice, pause for effect, use humour as appropriate; move around the podium – avoid the temptation to take refuge behind a lectern or table. Don't be afraid of silence – it's often necessary to allow your audience time to digest an argument or read a transparency.
- Be enthusiastic: enthusiasm excites interest and is infectious.
- Dress appropriately (i.e. in such a way as not to detract from what you have to say).
- Don't fidget with pens, car keys or loose change in your pocket.

Of course, if you are presenting in a language other than your first language, you may need to rely more on reading your script. In this case, it can be helpful to intersperse your reading with a few ad lib comments.

Obviously, delivering any kind of talk can be a nerve-racking business. Good preparation can reduce nerves as can relaxation exercises and having a glass of water at hand. (See Byron 1999, for useful tips on steadying nerves.)

9.3 Visual Aids

Visual aids, if used appropriately, can enhance an oral presentation by

1. helping an audience to follow your talk;
2. introducing meaningful distraction, i.e. variety.

For example, it often makes sense to show your audience the structure of your presentation at the beginning. This gives them an overview, a conceptual map, to guide them.

Whether your aids are transparencies on an Overhead Projector,

PowerPoint slides or multimedia presentations, the same general rules apply:

- Make sure that you are completely familiar with the technology (or have good technical support). Nothing spoils a presentation more than a technical hitch – especially if time is of the essence.
- If you plan to give an electronic presentation, always bring a hardcopy backup with you – just in case unforeseen technical problems arise. It also makes sense to check in advance with the organizers of the event to find out what version of a particular piece of software they have: if you arrive with a presentation saved in PowerPoint for Office 2000 and the organizers have only PowerPoint for Office 97, there may be compatibility problems.
- The information presented on each screen should be minimal and focus attention on the main point currently being made. One of the authors of this study recently attended a PowerPoint presentation in which the presenter's talk was reproduced verbatim on each screen. As human beings can read more quickly than they can speak, everyone had finished reading each screen before the presenter had finished speaking – a very distracting and unsatisfactory arrangement.
- Information presented on screen, slides or transparencies should be sufficiently large to be seen at the back of the hall. We recommend a minimum font size of 24.
- After showing each slide / transparency / screen, allow a few minutes' silence for the audience to read it.

A vital part of your preparation is the REHEARSAL. You can rehearse in front of a supportive fellow-student or colleague or in front of the mirror. But rehearse you must! It is the only way to establish exactly how long your presentation will take. As a rule of thumb one double-spaced A4 sheet takes three minutes to read, i.e. if you have transparencies to show, a 20-minute conference paper should be no longer than 6 pages. A rehearsal also gives you an opportunity to consider the best way to arrange your papers, where to stand and so on. A good rehearsal will also identify shortcomings in your presentation – whether in content or delivery.

A rehearsal is particularly important if you are giving your presentation in a language other than your mother tongue. The key to successfully delivering a paper in a foreign language is to *speak slowly*. You should arrange a rehearsal a week or two in advance of your presentation and rehearse in front of a native speaker of the language in which you are presenting. This will give you time to iron out any difficulties in your delivery.

A very useful exercise is to video yourself giving a talk. This helps you to identify your personal style and consider any improvements you could make. Do you smile enough / too much? Do you make enough eye contact with (all the members of) the audience? Do you speak at an appropriate speed / use appropriate intonation? Do you have any habits which detract from what you have to say? While some idiosyncracies – e.g. particular gestures when making important points – are charming, others – e.g. the constant removal and repositioning of glasses – can be most irritating.

Your preparation should also include some consideration of the *Question and Answer* session which will follow your presentation. This is where you can get valuable feedback on your work, so don't be afraid of constructive criticism.

Try to remain as calm and composed as possible. If you are asked a question which you can't answer, don't panic – you're not expected to be omniscient. Honesty is usually the best policy: admit that you don't know the answer and *either* promise to look into the matter and get back to the questioner *or* ask if anyone in the audience has any views on the matter.

Avoid confrontation: if you are asked a particularly hostile question, admit that there are other approaches / conclusions possible and offer to discuss these with the questioner after the session.

Finally, the ability to present your research orally is not only vital in disseminating the results of your research, it can also make an important contribution to your reputation and the development of your career. Practice does make perfect, so take every opportunity you can to hone this particular skill.

10. Assessing Your Research

Evaluation is a crucial part of the research process. Apart from your own self-assessment as you work and write, your report of your research results will of course be assessed by teachers and probably your fellow students, and then perhaps later, if it reaches a wider audience, by peer reviewers or referees, by readers, and by present and future colleagues. Giving and receiving critical feedback is an essential part of life in an academic community. This chapter takes a brief look at the kinds of criteria that are commonly used in research assessment, especially in the assessment of theses.

10.1 Self-assessment

The first assessment of your work takes place in your own head, each time you revise. Here is a checklist of the kinds of purely methodological issues you might want to assess in your own work, in addition to obvious matters like correct language, accurate documentation, and reader-friendliness.

- *Research question / aim.* Is it clearly stated? Have you explained why this is a good question / an important or interesting aim?
- *Other relevant research.* How well did you relate what you are doing to what others have done? Have you consulted the most relevant sources?
- *Hypothesis.* Are you starting or concluding with a specific hypothesis? Did you make this clear? What kind of hypothesis is it? Why is it interesting / important? Is it well justified?
- *Material.* Have you presented your empirical material clearly? Have you explained why you chose it? How relevant is it to your research question? Have you explained how you collected it? How representative is it?
- *Relation between variables.* What kind of relation are you looking for / do you think you have found? Between what variables, exactly? Is this clear to the reader?
- *Theoretical model.* Have you explained why you chose a particular theoretical model or approach / a particular variant of that model? What about other possibilities? Did you explain why you rejected those? Have you adapted the model at all? Why?

- *Central concepts and categories.* Are they adequately defined? Justified against alternative concepts, categories and definitions? What kind of categories? What kind of classification? Have you been explicit enough in presenting these?
- *Counter-evidence.* Have you considered any? Have you dealt with borderline cases adequately? Counter-arguments? Alternative explanations?
- *Reliability.* Is the analysis reliable? Explicit enough to be replicable? Are the calculations accurate? Classifications consistent? Statistics appropriate?
- *Validity.* Are the conclusions valid? Hypotheses supported or not? Adequate evidence? Logical argument? Is the evidence relevant to the original research problem? Do the conclusions link up with the introduction and the stated aim?
- *Follow-up.* Now what? Have you made some suggestions?
- *Implications.* So what? Have you considered these, in the conclusion?

10.2 Internal Assessment

Your teachers, examiners or critical readers will assess your work on standard academic criteria. These criteria have been mentioned either explicitly or implicitly in our earlier comments on revision, and in the checklist above. In a nutshell, we could say that the key question is this: are the readers convinced by what you are telling them? The more they are convinced, the higher their opinion will be.

Behind this question there lie various assumptions. Readers are more likely to feel impressed if:

- *you appear to be trustworthy*: you seem careful, honest, thorough, objective; your facts and calculations are correct, your sources are correctly acknowledged, your quotations accurate
- *you provide evidence that logically supports your claims*: the examples are relevant and representative, there is enough evidence, your arguments are rigorous, your concepts and claims are explicit enough
- *you respect their needs as readers*: you write with clarity, in a reader-friendly style; you communicate well
- *you are telling them something that changes their way of thinking*, i.e. it seems to them to be important and interesting, to have added value.

To illustrate how these assumptions appear in assessment criteria, here is a version of the assessment form that one of us (AC) uses when reading and grading MA theses. As I read, I take notes under each of these headings.

- Justification of topic, interest, relevance
- Definition of problem, basic hypothesis, aims
- Awareness and critical presentation of other relevant research;
- Choice and justification of theoretical framework
- Presentation and justification of methodology
- Presentation and justification of data
- Analysis and discussion of results, use of evidence, logic
- Validity of conclusions, self-critical awareness of the work's strengths and weaknesses
- Overall structure, stylistic aspects, academic conventions, clarity
- Originality, wider implications, significance.

10.3 External Assessment

When you submit your research for publication to a journal or publisher, your work will be assessed again. Assessment criteria are usually expressed explicitly in a journal's or publisher's *Guidelines for Authors* and implicitly in the articles / books they publish. Before submitting your research it therefore makes sense to check whether your contribution meets the particular criteria of the journal / publisher you are targeting, for instance with respect to subject matter or approach.

If you are submitting your research as part of a funding application, it is essential to obtain all the relevant information from the funding body. Criteria are extremely important here, too, as is the documentation required. Applications which are *complete*, *meet the criteria* and are *submitted on time* are much more likely to be accepted.

10.4 Typical Weaknesses

On the reverse side of the coin, we can list some of the typical weaknesses that occur, both in academic texts such as theses and also in articles and books submitted for publication. These are the kinds of things that referees draw attention to when recommending, or in fact *not* recommending, that something be published.

Length

Some texts are much too long. The main reasons for excessive length seem to be:

- *Topic too wide* – not sufficiently restricted or specific.
- *Irrelevance* – mostly in the introductory sections, which are often too long. Writers may start too far away from their actual topic, from too general a level, so that it takes e.g. 25 pages instead of 5 to put the reader in the picture and get to the point. There is no reason to elaborate at length on theoretical background that you are not going to use in the analysis itself, or that is irrelevant to your main point. Information merely for information's sake is a bad principle.
- *Repetition* – Any academic writing involves some repetition, with main points introduced, developed and then summarized. But too much is too much. Readers who are told the same things many times feel that their intelligence is underestimated.
- *Banalities* – Do not waste time and space saying things that your readers will certainly know anyway, because they are obvious. And do not waste time and space on mere trivialities: what you say should be worth saying!

Organization

This may be unclear, or illogical. The reader gets the impression that the writer cannot see the wood for the trees, so that the work lacks an overall awareness of what the point of the whole thing is and how the various sections fit together into a coherent whole. The relation between the title and the individual sections may be odd, for instance; the title or a heading may seem inappropriate altogether.

Review of the literature

The writer neglects some major relevant sources. The writer is un-critical of the sources used, or relies very heavily on one or two sources only, giving a biased picture of what others have done.

Methodology

- *Lack of explicitness* – The topic question (the aim) is too vague if it is formulated merely as e.g. 'to discuss X' or 'to analyze X'. Crucial terms are not explicitly defined. Necessary information about the material or method of analysis is missing.

- *Lack of evidence* – Claims are made with no evidence to back them up, so that they appear to be purely subjective. Conclusions are not justified by the analysis. There is simply not enough data to support the generalizations that are proposed.

- *Lack of a critical attitude* – Several definitions of terms are listed, for instance, but with no critical discussion, no argument to defend why one particular definition has been selected rather than others. Other studies in the same area are simply listed rather than evaluated. Methods are described with no critical comment, naively taken at face value, assumed to be perfect. Other scholars' poor inferences are adopted and copied with no critical reaction.

- *Lack of statistics* – In a quantitative study, necessary statistics are not used where they would be appropriate.

- *Lack of appropriate theory* – For instance, the theoretical section sometimes seems to have no connection to the analytical part, so that one wonders what the theoretical bit was actually for. Or the analysis seems to proceed merely at random, from one subjective impression to another, with no theoretical justification.

- *Lack of criteria for data selection* – The choice of data is not sufficiently motivated with respect to the research question. The reader wonders why the writer is looking at material X if the question at hand is Y.

- *No implications* – The conclusion is merely a summary; there is no awareness of the possible practical or theoretical implications of the work, how this kind of research might be continued. The conclusion does not answer the question 'So what?'

Logic

- *Conceptual confusion* – Concepts or terms are vague, slippery, used in more than one sense, ambiguous, undefined.

- *Non-like categories.* This means that a classification is set up in such a way that the categories are not in fact of the same kind, so that they are not mutually exclusive. Books might be illogically classified as red, religious or fat, for instance.

- *Lack of criteria for categories* – Categories are set up correctly, but we are not told explicitly what the crucial criteria are on the basis of which an item is assigned to a given category. Alternatively, there seems to be no reason *why* a given category is set up, no indication of some interesting generalization that it allows.

- *Circular argument* – Data are preselected in order to support a given argument. For some research topics the data should be randomly selected (albeit from within a given corpus).
- *Fallacious argument* – A general conclusion is drawn from a particular textual passage, for instance, but the passage is not first shown to be typical. General conclusions cannot be drawn from non-typical particulars. Another type of fallacious argument is where a writer seeks to explain the occurrence of X by hypothesizing a cause Y, but neglects to consider other variables apart from Y which might also cause X. One form of this fallacy is known as an attribution error: that is, an error in the attribution of causation. Here, you infer that a cause is internal to the agent (e.g. a cognitive factor, in the translator's mind) but neglect or underestimate possible external causes (such as the client's instructions).
- *Confusion of correlation and cause* – To say that A and B correlate is not to say that A causes B.

Style

- *Readability* is bad: lack of signposts, too much verbosity, sentences too long and complicated, too many parentheses and subclauses, poor punctuation.
- *Quotation* – Too much direct quotation, rather than paraphrase or discussion. The general impression here is that the work of other scholars has not been properly digested.
- *Examples* – Too many, or too few; or not representative.
- *No personal touch,* or personal opinion.

Added value

The research brings nothing new: no new information, no new data, no new way of looking at the question, no new answers, no new concepts, no new research methods, no new evidence that supports or weakens a hypothesis, no new theoretical contribution. This criticism might apply to a PhD thesis, or to a paper submitted for publication. In an undergraduate term paper or an MA thesis, the added-value criterion is obviously interpreted rather differently. Here, important values are the student's mastery of basic research methodology, the student's knowledge of the major work done on a given topic, and the student's ability to write good academic prose. These all mean added value for the student concerned.

Plagiarism

Plagiarism means taking ideas or passages of text from other authors without saying where they come from. Etymologically, the word goes back to the idea of kidnapping: taking something without permission, a kind of stealing. If you copy someone else's words, if you use their expressions, you are plagiarizing if you do not acknowledge your source. It is even plagiarizing if you use exactly the same words as someone else and give the source, but fail to indicate that you are indeed quoting. To be on the safe side, it is better either to quote properly (i.e. with quotation marks or indentation) or else paraphrase and report freely, in your own words with, of course, mention of the source. Plagiarism is a serious matter, with serious consequences; maybe even the end of an academic career.

10.5 Publication and after

A really good MA thesis might be turned into an article, for publication. Indeed, this might even be one criterion of a first-class thesis. Getting your work published is certainly one sign of its quality, especially if the journal or book series uses a referee system.

But the process of assessment does not stop there. If your work catches the attention of other scholars in your field, it may be reviewed. Other scholars may refer to it and cite you in their own research, critically or approvingly. You yourself may develop your ideas further, refining your argument and analysis, discovering new points of view.

In fact, the process never stops. Research is a journey with no ultimate end-point. But the travelling can be fun, especially in congenial company. We hope this short book has given you a sense of direction, a preliminary map, and maybe even a first compass.

Bon voyage! Hyvää matkaa! Go n-eirí an bóthar leat!

References

Aaltonen, Sirkku (1996) *Acculturation of the Other: Irish Milieux in Finnish Drama Translation*, Joensuu: Joensuu University Press.

Agular-Amat, Anna and Laura Santamaría (2000) 'Terminology Policies, Diversity and Minoritised Languages', in A. Chesterman *et al.* (eds), 73-84.

Anderman, Gunilla (1998) 'Drama Translation', in M. Baker (ed), 71-74.

Anholt, Robert R.H. (1994) *Dazzel 'em with Style: The Art of Oral Scientific Presentation*, New York: W.H. Freeman.

Arnold, Doug, Lorna Balkan, Siety Meijer, R. Lee Humphreys and Louisa Sadler (1994) *Machine Translation: An Introductory Guide*, Manchester & Oxford: NCC Blackwell.

Austermühl, Frank (2001) *Electronic Tools for Translators: Translation Practices Explained Vol. 2*, Manchester: St. Jerome.

Baker, Mona (1995) 'Corpora in Translation Studies: An Overview and Some Suggestions for Future Research', *Target* 7(2):223-243.

----- (ed) (1998) *Routledge Encyclopedia of Translation Studies*, London & New York: Routledge.

Ballard, Michel (1997) 'Créativité et traduction', *Target* 9(1):85-110.

Bandia, Paul (2000) 'Towards a History of Translation in a (Post)-Colonial Context: an African Perspective', in A. Chesterman *et al.* (eds), 353-362.

Bassnett, Susan (1991) *Translation Studies*, revised edition, London & New York: Routledge.

----- (1998) 'Researching Translation Studies: The Case for Doctoral Research', in Peter Bush and Kirsten Malmkjær (eds) *Rimbaud's Rainbow. Literary Translation in Higher Education*, Amsterdam & Philadelphia: John Benjamins, 105-118.

----- (2000) 'Theatre and Opera', in P. France (ed), 96-103.

----- and André Lefevere (eds) (1998) *Constructing Cultures: Essays on Literary Translation,* Cleveland & Philadelphia: Multilingual Matters.

----- and Harish Trivedi (eds) (1999) *Post-colonial Translation: Theory and Practice*, London: Routledge.

Biblia (1997) *Tradurre la Bibbia*, Firenze: Biblia.

Bly, Robert (1984) 'The Eight Stages of Translation', in William Frawley (ed) *Translation: Literary, Linguistic and Philosophical Perspectives*, Newark: University of Delaware Press & London: Associated University Presses, 67-89.

Boase-Beier, Jean and Michael Holman (eds) (1999) *The Practices of Literary Translation*, Manchester: St. Jerome.

Booth, Wayne C., Gregory G. Columb and Joseph M. Williams (1995) *The Craft of Research*, Chicago: Chicago University Press.

Bowker, Lynne, Michael Cronin, Dorothy Kenny, and Jennifer Pearson (eds) (1998) *Unity in Diversity? Current Trends in Translation Studies*, Manchester: St. Jerome.

----- Dorothy Kenny and Jennifer Pearson (eds) (1998) *Bibliography of Translation Studies*, Manchester: St. Jerome.

----- Dorothy Kenny and Jennifer Pearson (eds) (1999) *Bibliography of Translation Studies*, Manchester: St. Jerome.

----- (2000a) *Bibliography of Translation Studies*, Manchester: St. Jerome.

----- Dorothy Kenny and Jennifer Pearson (eds) (2000b) 'Towards a Methodology for Exploiting Specialized Target Language Corpora as Translation Resources', *International Journal of Corpus Linguistics*, 5(1):17-52.

----- (2002) *Computer-Aided Translation: A Practical Introduction*, Ottawa: University of Ottawa Press.

Buzan, Tony (1995) *The Mind Map Book*, revised edition, London: BBC Books.

Byron, Lynda (1999) *Being Successful in Presentations*, Dublin: Blackhall.

Cabré, M. Teresa (1999) *Terminology: Theory, Methods and Applications*, edited by Juan C. Sager and translated by Janet Ann DeCesaris, Amsterdam & Philadelphia: John Benjamins.

Cao, Deborah (1996) 'On Translational Language Competence', *Babel* 42(4): 231-238.

Carr, Silvana E., Roda Roberts, Aideen Dufour and Dini Steyn (eds) (1996) *The Critical Link: Interpreters in the Community,* Amsterdam: Benjamins.

Catford, J.C. (1965) *A Linguistic Theory of Translation*, London: Oxford University Press.

Chambers Concise Dictionary (1989), edited by Davidson, George W., M.A. Seaton and J. Simpson, Chambers: Cambridge.

Charniak, Eugene (1993) *Statistical Language Learning*, Cambridge, MA: MIT Press.

Cheng, Susan (2000) 'Globalizing an e-Commerce Web Site', in R. Sprung (ed), 29-42.

Chesterman, Andrew (ed) (1989) *Readings in Translation Theory,* Helsinki: Oy Finn Lectura Ab.

----- (1997) *Memes of Translation: The Spread of Ideas in Translation*

Theory, Amsterdam & Philadelphia: John Benjamins.

----- (1998) *Contrastive Functional Analysis*, Amsterdam & Philadelphia: John Benjamins.

----- (2000a) 'Empirical Research Methods in Translation Studies', *Erikoiskielet ja käännösteoria* (VAKKI-symposiumi XX) (27):9-22.

----- (2000b) 'A Causal Model for Translation Studies', in M. Olohan (ed), 15-27.

----- Natividad Gallardo San Salvador and Yves Gambier (eds) (2000) *Translation in Context*, Amsterdam & Philadelphia: Benjamins.

----- and Emma Wagner (2002) *Can Theory Help Translators?*, Manchester: St. Jerome.

Classe, Olive (ed) (2000) *Encyclopedia of Literary Translation into English*, 2 vols, London: Fitzroy Dearborn

Cronin, Michael (1996) *Translating Ireland*, Cork: Cork University Press.

----- (2000) *Across the Lines: Travel, Language and Translation*, Cork: Cork University Press.

De Beaugrande, Robert (1978) *Factors in a Theory of Poetic Translating*, Assen: Van Gorcum.

De Linde, Zoe and Neil Kay (1999) *The Semiotics of Subtitling*, Manchester: St. Jerome.

Delisle, Jean (1999) *Portraits de traducteurs*, Ottawa: University of Ottawa Press.

----- and Judith Woodsworth (eds) (1995) *Translators through History (Les Traducteurs dans l'histoire)*, Amsterdam & Philadelphia: John Benjamins / Paris: Editions Unesco.

----- and Hannelore Lee-Jahnke (eds) (1998) *Enseignement de la traduction et la traduction dans l'enseignement*, Ottawa: University of Ottawa Press.

Doherty, Monika (ed) (1996) 'Information Structure: A Key Concept for Translation Theory', Special Issue, *Linguistics* 34(3).

Dollerup, Cay (2000) '"Relay" and "Support" Translations', in A. Chesterman *et al.* (eds), 17-26.

----- and Vibeke Appel (eds) (1996) *Teaching Translation and Interpreting 3: New Horizons*, Amsterdam & Philadelphia: John Benjamins.

Englund Dimitrova, Birgitta and Kenneth Hyltenstam (eds) (2000) *Language Processing and Simultaneous Interpreting*, Amsterdam & Philadelphia: John Benjamins.

Esselink, Bert (2000) *A Practical Guide to Software Localization*, revised edition, Amsterdam & Philadelphia: John Benjamins.

Fairbairn, Gavin J. and Christopher Winch (1996) *Reading, Writing, and Reasoning: A Guide for Students*, Buckingham: The Society for Research into Higher Education and Open University Press.

Fawcett, Peter (2000) 'Translation in the Broadsheets', *The Translator* 6(2):295-307.

Fodor, István (1976) *Film Dubbing – Phonetic, Semiotic, Esthetic and Psychological Aspects,* Hamburg: Helmut Buske Verlag.

France, Peter (ed) (2000) *The Oxford Guide to Literature in English Translation*, New York: Oxford University Press.

Gaddis Rose, Marilyn (1997) *Translation and Literary Criticism*, Manchester: St. Jerome.

----- (ed) (2000) *Beyond the Western Tradition*, Translation Perspectives 11, CRIT: Binghamton.

Gambier, Yves (1994) 'La retraduction, tour et retour', *Meta* 39(3):413-417.

----- (1998) *Translating for the Media*, Turku: Centre for Translation and Interpreting.

----- Daniel Gile and Christopher Taylor (eds) (1997) *Conference Interpreting: Current Trends in Research*, Amsterdam & Philadelphia: John Benjamins.

----- and Henrik Gottlieb (eds) (2001) *Multimedia Translation*, Amsterdam & Philadelphia: John Benjamins.

Gémar, Jean-Claude (1995) *Traduire, ou, L'art d'interpréter: langue, droit et société: éléments de jurilinguistique*, Quebec: Presses de l'Université du Québec.

Gile, Daniel (1995) *Basic Concepts and Models for Interpreter and Translator Training*, Amsterdam & Philadelphia: John Benjamins.

----- (1998) 'Observational Studies and Experimental Studies in the Investigation of Conference Interpreting', *Target* 10(1):69-98.

-----, Helle Dam, Friedel Dubslaff and Anne Schjoldager (eds) (2001) *Getting Started in Interpreting Research*, Amsterdam & Philadelphia: John Benjamins.

Gillham, Bill (2000a) *Case Study Research Methods*, London & New York: Continuum.

----- (2000b) *Developing a Questionnaire*, London & New York: Continuum.

----- (2000c) *The Research Interview*, London & New York: Continuum.

Gregory, Michael (2001) 'What can Linguistics Learn from Translation?', in Erich Steiner and Colin Yallop (eds) *Exploring Translation and Multilingual Text Production: Beyond Content*, Berlin: Mouton de Gruyter, 19-40.

Gutt, Ernst-August (2000) *Translation and Relevance*, Manchester: St. Jerome.

Hall, P.A.V. and R. Hudson (eds) (1997) *Software without Frontiers, a Multiplatform, Multicultural, Multination Approach*, Chichester: John Wiley.

Hansen, Gyde (ed) (1999) *Probing the Process in Translation: Methods and Results*, Copenhagen Studies in Language 24, Copenhagen: Samfundslitteratur.

Hatim, Basil (2001) *Teaching and Researching Translation*, London & New York: Longman.

----- and Ian Mason (1990) *Discourse and the Translator*, London & New York: Longman.

Hempel, Carl (1952) *Fundamentals of Concept Formation in Empirical Science*, Chicago: University of Chicago Press.

Herbst, Thomas (1994) *Linguistische Aspekte der Synchronisation von Fernsehserien*, Tübingen: Max Niemeyer.

Hermans, Theo (1999) *Translation in Systems: Descriptive and System-oriented Approaches Explained*, Manchester: St. Jerome.

Hofstadter, Douglas R. (1997) *Le ton beau de Marot*, New York: Basic Books.

Holmes, James S. (1994) *Translated! Papers on Literary Translation and Translation Studies*, 2nd Edition, Amsterdam: Rodopi.

House, Juliane (1997) *Translation Quality Assessment. A Model Revisited*, Tübingen: Gunter Narr.

Huhtala, Paula (1995) *Från teori till praktik: analys av översättningar från finska till svenska*, Oulu: Oulu University.

Ivarsson, Jan (1992) *Subtitling for the Media*, Stockholm: Transedit.

Jääskeläinen, Riitta (1999) *Tapping the Process: An Explorative Study of the Cognitive and Affective Factors Involved in Translating*, Joensuu: University of Joensuu.

Jasper, David (1993) *Translating Religious Texts: Translation, Transgression, and Interpretation*, New York: St. Martin's Press.

Johnsen, Åse (2000) 'El mundo de [la filo]sofia', in A. Chesterman *et al.* (eds), 317-326.

Johnston, David (ed) (1996) *Stages of Translation*, Bath: Absolute Classics.

Kaltenbacher, Martin (2000) 'Aspects of Universal Grammar in Human versus Machine Translation', in A. Chesterman *et al.* (eds) 221-230.

Kelly, Dorothy (2000) 'Text Selection for Developing Translator Competence: Why Texts from the Tourist Sector Constitute Suitable Material', in C. Schäffner and B. J. Adab (eds), 157-167.

Kenny, Dorothy (1999) 'CAT Tools in an Academic Environment: What are they good for?', *Target* 11(1):65-82.

----- (2001) *Lexis and Creativity in Translation: A Corpus-based Study*, Manchester: St. Jerome.

Kiraly, Don (1995) *Pathways to Translation: Pedagogy and Process*, Kent, Ohio: Kent State University Press.

----- (2000) *A Social Constructivist Approach to Translator Education*, Manchester: St. Jerome.

Klingberg, Göte (1986) *Children's Fiction in the Hands of Translators*, Lund: LiberFörlag.

Kohlmayer, Rainer (1994) 'Übersetzung als ideologische Anpassung: Oscar Wildes Gesellschaftskomödien mit nationalsozialistischer Botschaft', in M. Snell-Hornby *et al.* (eds), 91-101.

Koskinen, Kaisa (2000) *Beyond Ambivalence: Postmodernity and the Ethics of Translation*, Tampere: Tampere University Press.

Kuhiwczak, Piotr (1999) 'Translation and Language Games in the Balkans', in Gunilla Anderman and Margaret Rogers (eds) *Word, Text, Translation. Liber Amicorum for Peter Newmark*, Clevedon: Multilingual Matters, 217-224.

Krings, Hans P. (1986) *Was in den Köpfen von Übersetzern vorgeht: Eine empirische Untersuchung zur Struktur des Übersetzun-gsprozesses an fortgeschrittenen Französischlernern*, Tübingen: Gunter Narr.

Kussmaul, Paul (1995) *Training the Translator*, Amsterdam & Philadelphia: John Benjamins.

----- and Sonja Tirkkonen-Condit (1995) 'Think-Aloud Protocol Analysis in Translation Studies', *TTR* 8(1):177-199.

Lambert, José (1996) 'Language and Translation as General Management Problems', in C. Dollerup and V. Appel (eds), 271-294.

Laviosa, Sara (1998) 'Core Patterns of Lexical Use in a Comparable Corpus of English Narrative Prose', *Meta* 43(4):557-570.

Lefevere, André (1992) *Translation/ History/ Culture: A Sourcebook*, London & New York: Routledge.

Leigh, Andrew and Michael Maynard (1999) *The Perfect Presentation*, London: Random House.

Leppihalme, Ritva (2000) 'Foreignizing Strategies in Drama Translation. The Case of the Finnish *Oleanna*', in A. Chesterman *et al.* (eds), 153-162.

Leuven-Zwart, Kitty van (1989) 'Translation and Original: Similarities and Dissimilarities, I', *Target* 1(2):151-181.

----- (1990) 'Translations and Original: Similarities and Dissimilarities, II', *Target* 2(1):69-95.

Lewis, Jack P. (1981) *The English Bible from KJV to NIV: A History and Evaluation*, Grand Rapids, MI: Baker Books.

Lindfors, A-M. (2001) 'Respect or Ridicule: Translation Strategies and the Images of A Foreign Culture', *Helsinki English Studies* [online], I. Available from: http://www.eng.helsinki.fi/hes/Translation [Accessed 12 July 2001]

Luyken, Georg-Michael (1991) *Overcoming Language Barriers in Television: Dubbing and Subtitling for the European Audience*, Manchester: The European Institute for the Media.

Maier, Carol (1998) 'Reviewing and Criticism', in M. Baker (ed), 205-210.

Marc, P. (19 July 2001) 'Can MT rival HT?', *FLEFO* [online]. Available from: http://forums.compuserve.com [Accessed 30 July 2001]

Mason, Ian (2000) 'Models and Methods in Dialogue Interpreting Research', in M. Olohan (ed), 215-231.

----- (ed) (2001) *Triadic Exchanges: Studies in Dialogue Interpreting*, Manchester: St. Jerome.

Melby, Alan K with C. Terry Warner (1995) *The Possibility of Language: A Discussion of Language with Implications for Human and Machine Translation*, Amsterdam & Philadelphia: John Benjamins.

Merkel, Magnus (1998) 'Consistency and Variation in Technical Translations. A Study of Translators' Attitudes', in L. Bowker *et al.* (eds), 137-150.

Meta (1998) 'L'approche basée sur le corpus/The Corpus-based Approach', Special Issue 43(4).

Meta (2001) 'Evaluation: paramètres, méthodes, aspects pédago-giques', Special Issue 46(2).

Morris, Marshall (ed) (1995) *Translation and the Law*, Amsterdam & Philadelphia: John Benjamins.

Mossop, Brian (1994) 'Goals and Methods for a Course in Translation Theory', in M. Snell-Hornby *et al.* (eds), 401-410.

----- (2000) 'The Workplace Procedures of Professional Translators', in A. Chesterman *et al.* (eds), 39-48.

Munday, Jeremy (2001) *Introducing Translation Studies: Theories and Applications*, London & New York: Routledge.

Nida, Eugene A. (1964) *Toward a Science of Translating: with Special Reference to Principles and Procedures Involved in Bible Translating*, Leiden: E.J. Brill.

----- and Charles R.Taber (1969) *The Theory and Practice of Translation*, Leiden: E.J.Brill.

Nord, Christiane (1991) *Text Analysis in Translation: Theory, Methodology and Didactic Application*, Amsterdam: Rodopi.

----- (1997) *Translating as a Purposeful Activity: Functionalist Approaches Explained*, Manchester: St. Jerome.

Oakes, Michael P. (1998) *Statistics for Corpus Linguistics*, Edinburgh: Edinburgh University Press.

O'Connell, Eithne M.T. (1994) 'Media Translation and Lesser-Used Languages: Implications of Subtitles for Irish Language Broadcasting', in Frederico Eguíluz, Raquel Merino, Vickie Olsen, Eterío Pajares and José Miguel Santamaría (eds) *Transvases Culturales: Literatura, Cine, Traducción*, Vitoria: Facultad de Filologia, 367-374.

----- (1998) 'Choices and Constraints in Screen Translation', in L. Bowker *et al.* (eds), 65-71.

Oittinen, Riitta (1993) *I am me, I am other: on the Dialogics of Translating for Children*, Tampere: University of Tampere.

Olohan, Maeve (ed) (2000) *Intercultural Faultlines. Research Models in Translation Studies I. Textual and Cognitive Aspects*, Manchester: St. Jerome.

----- and Mona Baker (2000) 'Reporting *that* in Translated English. Evidence for Subconscious Processes of Explicitation?', *Across* (1)2:141-158.

Palimpsestes (1990) 'Retraduire', Issue No. 4.

Pearson, Jennifer (1998) *Terms in Context*, Amsterdam & Philadelphia: John Benjamins.

----- (1999) 'Genes Go Wild in the Countryside: Using Corpora to Improve Translation', *Teanga* 18:71-83.

Pelegrin, Benito (ed) (1987) 'La traduction: reflections reflets', *SUD* 69-70, Special Issue.

Phelan, Mary (2001) *The Interpreter's Resource*, Cleveland: Multilingual Matters.

Popovič, Anton (1970) 'The Concept "Shift of Expression" in Translation Analysis', in James Holmes (ed), *The Nature of Translation: Essays on the Theory and Practice of Literary Translation*, The Hague & Paris: Mouton, 78-87.

Puurtinen, Tiina (1995) *Linguistic Acceptability in Children's Literature*, Joensuu: University of Joensuu Press.

Pym, Anthony (1997) *Pour une éthique du traducteur*, Ottawa: Presses de l'Université d'Ottawa.

----- (1998) *Method in Translation History*, Manchester: St. Jerome.

Robinson, Douglas (ed) (1997a) *Western Translation Theory from Herodotus to Nietzsche*, Manchester: St. Jerome.

----- (1997b) *Translation and Empire: Postcolonial Theories Explained*, Manchester: St. Jerome.

Rosch, Eleanor and Barbara B. Lloyd (eds) (1978) *Cognition and Categorization*, Hillsdale, NJ: Erlbaum.

Rushdie, Salman (1991) *Imaginary Homelands. Essays and Criticism 1981-1991*, London: Granta.

Sager, Juan C. (1990) *A Practical Course in Terminology Processing*, Amsterdam & Philadelphia: John Benjamins.

----- (1993) *Language Engineering and Translation. Consequences of Automation*, Amsterdam & Philadelphia: John Benjamins.

Šarčević, Susan (1997) *New Approach to Legal Translation*, The Hague: Kluwer Law International.

Schäffner, Christina (ed) (1998) *Translation and Quality*, Clevedon: Multilingual Matters.

----- and Beverly Joan Adab (eds) (2000) *Developing Translation Competence*, Amsterdam & Philadelphia: John Benjamins.

Schäler, Reinhard. (1998) 'The Problem with Machine Translation', in L. Bowker *et al.* (eds), 151-156.

Scott, Michael (2001) *Wordsmith Tools 3.0*, Oxford: Oxford University Press.

Shlesinger, Miriam and Franz Pöchhacker (2001) *The Interpreting Studies Reader*, London: Routledge.

Shuttleworth, Mark and Moira Cowie (1997) *Dictionary of Translation Studies*, Manchester: St. Jerome.

Snell-Hornby, Mary (1989) 'Andere Länder, andere Sitten. Zum Problem der kulturbedingten Interferenz in der Translation', in Heide Schmidt (ed) *Interferenz in der Translation*, Leipzig: VEB Verlag Enzyklopädie, 135-143.

----- Franz Pöchhacker and Klaus Kaindl (eds) (1994) *Translation Studies: An Interdiscipline. Selected papers from the Translation Studies Congress, Vienna, 9-12 September 1992*, Amsterdam: John Benjamins.

Sorvali, Irma (1998) 'The Translator as Creative Being with special regard to the Translation of Literature and LSP', *Babel* 44(3):234-243.

Sprung, Robert C. (ed) (2000) *Translating into Success*, Amsterdam & Philadelphia: John Benjamins.

Steiner, Erich (1998) 'A Register-Based Translation Evaluation: An Advertisement as a Case in Point', *Target* 10(2):291-318.

Stubbs, Michael (1986) 'Lexical Density: A Technique and Some Findings', in Malcolm Coulthard (ed) *Talking about Text*, Discourse

Analysis Monograph No.13, English Language Research, Birmingham: University of Birmingham, 27-42.

----- (1996) *Text and Corpus Analysis: Computer-assisted Studies of Language and Culture*, Oxford and Cambridge, MA: Blackwell.

Susam-Sarajeva, Şebnem (2001) 'Is One Case Always Enough?', *Perspectives in Translatology* 9(3):167-176.

----- (forthcoming b) 'Multiple-entry Visa for Travelling Theory: Retranslations of Literary and Cultural Theories', *Target*.

Swales, John (1991) *Genre Analysis*, Cambridge: Cambridge University Press.

Target (1995) 'Interpreting Research', Special Issue 7(1).

Translation Journal (2001), issue 5(3), http://www.accurapid.com/journal/.

The Translator (1999) 'Dialogue Interpreting', Special Issue 5(2).

The Translator (2000) 'Evaluation and Translation', Special Issue 6(2).

The Translator (2001) 'The Return to Ethics', Special Issue 7(2).

Tirkkonen-Condit, Sonja and Riitta Jääskeläinen (eds) (2000) *Tapping and Mapping the Processes of Translation and Interpreting: Outlooks on Empirical Research*, Amsterdam & Philadelphia: John Benjamins.

Toury, Gideon (1995) *Descriptive Translation Studies and Beyond*, Amsterdam & Philadelphia: John Benjamins.

Trosborg, Anna (ed) (1997) *Text Typology and Translation*, Amsterdam & Philadelphia: John Benjamins.

TTR (1989) 'L'erreur en traduction', Special Issue 2(2).

Tymoczko, Maria (1999) *Translation in a Postcolonial Context: Early Irish Literature in English Translation*, Manchester: St. Jerome.

Upton, Carole-Anne (ed) (2000) *Moving Target. Theatre Translation and Cultural Relocation*, Manchester: St. Jerome.

Vanderplank, Robert (1999) 'Global Medium – Global Resource? Perspectives and Paradoxes in Using Authentic Broadcast Material for Teaching and Learning English', in Claus Gutzmann (ed) *Teaching and Learning English as a Global Language: Native and Non-Native Perspectives*, Tübingen: Stauffenberg, 253-266.

Venuti, Lawrence (1995a) *The Translator's Invisibility: A History of Translation*, London & New York: Routledge.

----- (1995b) 'Translation, Authorship, Copyright', *The Translator* 1(1):1-24.

----- (1998) *The Scandals of Translation: Towards an Ethics of Difference*, London: Routledge.

Vermeer, Hans J. (1996) *A Skopos Theory of Translation*, Heidelberg: TEXTconTEXT.

Vinay, Jean-Paul and Jean Darbelnet (1958) *Stylistique comparée du français et de l'anglais*, Paris: Didier.

----- (1995) *Comparative Stylistics of French and English: A Methodology for Translation*, trans. of Vinay and Darbelnet (1958) by Juan C. Sager and Marie-Josée Hamel, Amsterdam & Philadelphia: John Benjamins.

Von Flotow, Luise (1997) *Translation and Gender: Translating in the 'Era of Feminism'*, Manchester & Ottawa: St. Jerome & Ottawa University Press.

Von Wright, Georg H. (1971) *Explanation and Understanding*, London: Routledge and Kegan Paul.

Wadensjö, Cecilia (1998) *Interpreting as Interaction*, London: Longman.

Waldrop, M. Mitchell (1994) *Complexity*, Harmondsworth: Penguin Books.

Whitman-Linsen, Candace (1992) *Through the Dubbing Glass: The Synchronization of American Motion Pictures into German, French and Spanish*, Frankfurt am Main: Peter Lang.

Woods, Anthony, Paul Fletcher, and Arthur Hughes (1986) *Statistics in Language Studies*, Cambridge: Cambridge University Press.

Wright, Sue Ellen and Gerhard Budin (eds) (1997) *Handbook of Terminology Management, Vol.1: Basic Aspects of Terminology Management*, Amsterdam & Philadelphia: John Benjamins.

----- (2001) *Handbook of Terminology Management, Vol. II: Application-oriented Terminology Management*, Amsterdam & Philadelphia: John Benjamins.

Wright, Sue Ellen and Leland D.Wright Jr. (eds) (1993) *Scientific and Technical Translation*, American Translators Association Scholarly Monograph Series, vol. 4, Amsterdam& Philadelphia: John Benjamins.

Yin, Robert K. (1994) *Case Study Research: Design and Methods*, 2nd edition, Applied Social Research Method Series, Vol. 5, Thousand Oaks: Sage.

Zanettin, Frederico (2000) 'Parallel Corpora in Translation Studies. Issues

Subject Index

Allusion 6, 87
Annotated translation 7
Assessment 8, 63, 122-124, 128
   (Translation) Quality Assessment 1, 8, 23, 56, 77, 86, 91
   Research assessment 122
   Self-assessment 122
   Trainee assessment 27
BA 1f., 21, 38-40
Best practice 24, 91
Bibliography 4, 34, 44, 91 f.
Case study 9, 15, 19, 65 f., 78
Category 59, 65, 94 f., 106, 115, 123, 126f.
   Categorization 11, 94
Cause 53-57, 61, 70, 76f., 84, 86, 110, 112, 127
   Causation 54, 80
Claim 3, 18, 62, 64-69, 71-82, 92f., 96, 103, 105-107, 109-111,
   114, 123, 126
Classification 20f., 53, 59, 74, 95, 123, 126
Comparable texts 7f., 70, 85, 90, 92
Corpus 13, 20 f., 23, 30, 33, 41, 51, 65-68, 92, 98f., 127
Corpus-based Translation Studies 7, 16, 38, 40f., 66
Correlation 51, 84, 114, 127
Correspondence 7, 50, 91
Cultural Turn 18, 56
Data 2, 4, 23, 27, 33, 46, 57f., 63, 66, 69, 71-73, 77f., 80 f., 90-97,
   100, 104, 107f., 114, 118, 124, 126f.
Effect 15, 22, 53-55, 57, 70, 76f., 86f., 110, 112, 119
   Translation effects 8, 16, 18, 54-56, 77
Equivalence 8, 21, 49-51, 53, 55, 69, 74, 90
Ethics 1, 18-20, 22, 26f.
Explicitation 6 f., 53, 66
Feedback 4, 26, 42, 55, 114, 121f.
Hypothesis 2, 4, 24, 56, 58, 62 f., 66, 68 f., 72 f., 75-82, 91, 93f.,
   109, 111, 117, 122, 124, 127
   Descriptive 75-77, 79
   Explanatory 66, 76f.
   General 62, 93
   Interpretive 73-75, 80, 82, 94f.
   Predictive 56, 77

Hypothesis-testing 63, 66, 68, 77-79, 81f., 93, 117
Ideology 54, 56, 60, 86, 88, 90
Interpreting 1, 21-23, 30, 62f., 75
Interview 8, 10, 16, 23-25, 62, 65, 67, 69, 76, 91f.
Journals 21, 27, 30f., 34, 36f., 104, 124, 128
Language planning 21, 68
Legal translation 13
Lexical density 85f., 99
Literary translation 4, 8, 9, 11, 16, 70, 76f., 88
    Children's literature 9, 12, 76, 93, 112
    Drama 9
    Poetry 9f., 64
    (Prose) fiction 9f., 81, 88
Literature review/search/survey 4, 46, 69, 91f., 101, 125
MA (Masters) 1, 21, 39, 116, 124, 127f.
Meta-analysis 91f.
Methodology 2, 7, 20, 28, 33, 42, 65 f., 81, 107f., 118, 122, 124,
    126, 128
Mind map 32, 69, 107
Model 20, 25, 38, 40, 48-53, 57, 60, 122
    Causal 49, 53, 55f.
    Comparative 49-51, 53
    Process 49, 51-53
    Research 2
    Theoretical 48f., 95, 122
Multilingual documentation 12, 24, 26
Multimedia translation 1, 13f., 44
Non-translated texts 7, 51, 53, 66, 70, 76, 85, 87, 90, 92
Norms 13, 16, 18, 54-56, 74, 86-88
Note-taking 22, 31f., 34, 101, 105
Parallel texts 7, 24
PhD 1, 39f., 91, 116, 127
Plagiarism 32, 128
Planning 4, 28, 42-45, 114
    Research Plan 4, 28, 46, 70, 109
Polysystem 16, 56
Protocol studies 25, 56, 88f.
    Think-aloud protocol 25, 63, 91f.
Questionnaire 9, 15 f., 24, 62 f., 67, 69, 91f.
Quotations 32, 103 f., 123, 127f.
Random selection 93, 96

Reception 10 f., 17, 56, 86, 88, 118
References 32, 34-37, 101-103, 106, 113
Religious texts 11
Representativeness 41, 65, 79, 92-94, 96, 112, 114, 122f., 127
Research
  Applied 3, 13, 67f.
  Conceptual 18, 20, 58f., 73
  Empirical 58-60, 62, 65, 73, 75, 84, 89f., 96, 107
  Qualitative 64f.
  Quantitative 7, 64f., 98
Research diary 45, 107
Research methods 46, 58, 60, 63, 65, 67, 90, 127
Research question 4, 29, 45f., 67, 69, 71-76, 90, 92, 113, 117f.,
    122, 126f.
Research report 5, 29, 57, 72, 91, 101, 104, 107f., 122
Research topic 6, 10, 13, 15, 24, 26-28, 69, 92, 126f.
Retranslation 40, 71-74, 77f., 81, 93
Reviews 8, 17, 55, 86, 91f., 99
Shift 6, 22, 50f., 53, 78, 111
Simplification 66
Skopos theory 9, 55
Software 12, 14-16, 25, 44, 66, 98, 120
  Software Localization 15, 26, 45
Standardization 20, 56, 111
Statistics 65, 79, 96, 99, 123, 126
Study
  Experimental 63f.
  Observational 62
  Pilot 66, 92
  Survey 67
Supervisor 39, 41f., 46, 104f., 108, 114
Technical translation 9, 12, 76
Terminology 1, 13f., 20 f., 26, 30, 45, 50, 68, 90, 115
Text analysis 1, 6-8, 39f., 44, 90
Text type 13f., 70, 75, 85, 90, 93, 99 111
Theoretical framework 59, 92, 107, 124
Tourism texts 9, 12
Translation criticism 11, 56
Translation evaluation 36, 40, 52
Translation history 1f., 16-18, 28f., 118
Translation memory 14f., 24, 26, 45

Translation process 1, 7, 9, 15, 23 f., 48, 54, 63
Translation profession 1 f., 14, 19, 26 f., 31, 38, 40, 62f., 67f., 70,
    76
Translation strategy 6, 12, 17, 37, 50, 52f., 87, 90, 98
Translation technology 1, 14-16, 26
Translation with commentary 7f., 39f.
Translators' footnotes 10, 24, 76, 87, 96
Translator's preface 10, 24, 72, 91, 96
Translator training 1, 6, 12f., 16, 24-27, 68
TRANSLOG 52, 62f.
Triangulation 63
Variables 65, 83-87, 89, 122, 127
  Context variables 53, 83-88
  Text variables 84-89
Website translation 15, 26
WordSmith 98f.
Workplace studies 15, 23, 26, 62, 92

Author Index

Aaltonen, Sirkku   10
Adab, Beverly Joan   26, 68
Agular-Amat, Anna   68
Anderman, Gunilla   10, 36
Anholt, Robert R.H.   117
Appel, Vibeke   27
Arnold, Doug   14
Austermühl, Frank   16
Baker, Mona   4, 18, 66, 86f., 103
Ballard, Michel   59
Bandia, Paul   88
Bassnett, Susan   9-11, 18
Bly, Robert   8, 10
Boase-Beier, Jean   9
Booth, Wayne C.   28, 101, 110, 112
Bowker, Lynne   4, 13, 15, 35, 38, 66
Brecht, Bertolt   9
Budin, Gerhard   21
Buzan, Tony   32, 70
Byron, Lynda   119
Cabré, M. Teresa   21
Cao, Deborah   91
Carr, Silvana E.   22
Catford, J.C.   49, 102
Charniak, Eugene   100
Chekov, Anton   9
Cheng, Susan   15
Chesterman, Andrew   2, 4, 7, 9, 16, 49, 54, 60
Classe, Olive   4
Cowie, Moira   4, 7, 16
Cronin, Michael   12, 18, 74
Darbelnet, Jean   49
De Beaugrande, Robert   10
De Linde, Zoe   14
Delisle, Jean   17, 27
Doherty, Monika   76
Dollerup, Cay   27, 59
Doyle, Roddy   40
Englund, Dimitrova   22

Esselink, Bert   15
Fairbairn, Gavin J.   34
Fawcett, Peter   8, 11
Fodor, István   13
Freud, Sigmund   108
Gaarder, Jostein   87
Gaddis Rose, Marilyn   9, 11
Gambier, Yves   14, 22, 72
Gémar, Jean-Claude   13
Gile, Daniel   22, 33, 58, 60, 63, 75, 102
Gillham, Bill   1, 45, 65, 91, 102
Gottlieb, Henrik   14
Gregory, Michael   11
Gutt, Ernst-August   56
Hall, P.A.V.   15
Hansen, Gyde   25, 62
Hatim, Basil   2, 27, 31, 35, 102
Hempel, Carl   60-62, 102
Herbst, Thomas   13
Hermans, Theo   56, 82, 102
Hofstadter, Douglas R.   64f., 89
Holman, Michael   9
Holmes, James S.   10
House, Juliane   8
Hudson, R.   15
Huhtala, Paula   76
Hyltenstam, Birgitta   22
Hyltenstam, Kenneth   22
Ivarsson, Jan   14
Jääskeläinen, Riitta   25, 56, 64, 76, 88f., 91
Jasper, David   11
Johnsen, Åse   87
Johnston, David   10
Kaindl, Klaus   37
Kaltenbacher, Martin   86
Kay, Neil   14
Kelly, Dorothy   12
Kenny, Dorothy   15, 67, 99, 103
Kiraly, Don   16, 26
Klingberg, Göte   12
Kohlmayer, Rainer   17

Koskinen, Kaisa   20
Krings, Hans P.   52
Kuhiwczak, Piotr   36
Kussmaul, Paul   25f.
Lambert, José   24
Laviosa, Sara   51, 102
Lee-Jahnke, Hannelore   27
Lefevere, André   9, 11, 16
Leigh, Andrew   117
Leppihalme, Ritva   56, 66
Leuven-Zwart, Kitty van   7f., 51
Lewis, Jack P.   11
Lindfors, A-M.   37
Lloyd, Barbara B.   95
Luyken, Georg-Michael   13
Maier, Carol   8
Marc, P.   38
Mason, Ian   22, 35
Maynard, Michael   117
Melby, Alan K.   20
Merkel, Magnus   15
Morris, Marshall   13
Mossop, Brian   24, 37, 52, 62, 68
Munday, Jeremy   4, 35, 102
Nida, Eugene A.   11, 55, 102f.
Nord, Christiane   6, 52, 55
Oakes, Michael P.   100
O'Connell, Eithne   13f.
Oittinen, Riitta   12
Okara, Gabriel   88
Olohan, Maeve   4, 7, 67, 86f.
Pearson, Jennifer   13, 21
Pelegrin, Benito   10
Phelan, Mary   19
Pöchhacker, Franz   22, 37
Popovič, Anton   51
Puurtinen, Tiina   12, 91
Pym, Anthony   16, 20, 54, 91
Robinson, Douglas   16, 18, 19
Rogers, Margaret   36
Rosch, Eleanor   95

Rushdie, Salman 60
Sager, Juan C. 21, 52
Santamaría, Laura 68
Šarcević, Susan 13
Schäffner, Christina 8, 26, 68
Schäler, Reinhard 16
Scott, Michael 98
Shakespeare, William 74
Shlesinger, Miriam 22
Shuttleworth, Mark 4, 7, 16
Snell-Hornby, Mary 12, 37, 102
Sorvali, Irma 91
Sprung, Robert C. 24, 91
Steiner, Erich 36
Stubbs, Michael 99
Susam-Sarajeva, Şebnem 65, 73
Swales, John 9
Taber, Charles R. 11
Tirkkonen-Condit, Sonja 25, 56, 64, 91
Toury, Gideon 8, 32, 54, 56, 60, 90, 102
Trivedi, Harish 18
Trosborg, Anna 9
Twain, Mark 116
Tymoczko, Maria 93
Upton, Carole-Anne 10
Vanderplank, Robert 14
Venuti, Lawrence 18f.
Vermeer, Hans J. 9, 55
Vinay, Jean-Paul 49
Von Flotow, Luise 18
Von Wright, Georg H. 58
Wadensjö, Cecilia 22
Wagner, Emma 2, 67
Waldrop, M. Mitchell 74
Whitman-Linsen, Candace 13
Wilde, Oscar 17
Winch, Christopher 34
Woods, Anthony 96, 100
Woodsworth, Judith 17
Wright, Leland D. Jr. 13
Wright, Sue Ellen 13, 21

Yin, Robert K.   46, 65, 102
Zanettin, Frederico   66f., 92

St. Jerome Publishing
2 Maple Road West
Brooklands
Manchester
M23 9HH
UK

Tel. +44 (0)161 973 9856
Fax +44 (0)161 905 3498

stjerome@compuserve.com
www.stjerome.co.uk